Mirja Meyborg

The role of German universities in a system of joint knowledge generation and innovation

A social network analysis of publications and patents with a focus on the spatial dimension

The role of German universities in a system of joint knowledge generation and innovation

A social network analysis of publications and patents with a focus on the spatial dimension

by
Mirja Meyborg

KIT Scientific Publishing

Dissertation, Karlsruher Institut für Technologie (KIT)
Fakultät für Wirtschaftswissenschaften
Tag der mündlichen Prüfung: 20. Juni 2013
Referent: Prof. Dr. Jan S. Kowalski, Prof. Dr. Knut Koschatzky

Impressum

KIT Scientific Publishing

Karlsruher Institut für Technologie (KIT)
KIT Scientific Publishing
Straße am Forum 2
D-76131 Karlsruhe

KIT Scientific Publishing is a registered trademark of Karlsruhe Institute of Technology. Reprint using the book cover is not allowed.

www.ksp.kit.edu

Print on Demand 2013

ISBN 978-3-7315-0085-8

The role of German universities in a system of joint knowledge generation and innovation - A social network analysis of publications and patents with a focus on the spatial dimension

Zur Erlangung des akademischen Grades eines

Doktors der Wirtschaftswissenschaften

(Dr. rer. pol.)

der Fakultät für Wirtschaftswissenschaften
des Karlsruher Instituts für Technologie (KIT)

genehmigte

DISSERTATION

von

Dipl.-Ök. Mirja Meyborg

Referent: Prof. Dr. Jan S. Kowalski
Korreferent: Prof. Dr. Knut Koschatzky

Mündliche Prüfung: 20.06.2013 in Karlsruhe

Abstract

There is broad consensus that universities play a key role as knowledge platform in regional economic development. This PhD thesis exactly picks up this line of thought and explores the role of the German universities in a system of joint knowledge generation and innovation. The overall aim of this PhD thesis is to provide new insight into the German universities' behavioural patterns regarding their knowledge generation, innovation and collaboration function in order to finally provide appropriate policy recommendations which are very closely tailored to the requirements of the German universities as well as to the needs of the German knowledge-based community.

For this purpose, the thesis applies a broad social network analysis (SNA) of publications and patents that can make use of several thousand publications for each German university for a time period of ten years. The basic research lines are as follows.

First, it is explored which recent trends can be identified concerning university-university interactions as well as cooperations between universities and other actors in the research system (e.g. research institutes and industry). Second, it is shown how strong the German universities are already linked within these networks and to what extent they are important as a mediator in the transmission of information through the network. Third, the question whether the importance of the spatial factor has changed over time is tackled. Here, the development of the spatial dispersion of all German university cooperation partners is calculated in order to show if spatial proximity still matters greatly.

The empirical results confirm a highly increasing importance of collaboration activity in terms of publications and patent applications and point to a more dynamic development regarding university-industry linkages. It is further confirmed that the networks of the German universities have become much larger, and that the German universities have become more important as intermediary in the transmission of information through the network. A third central finding points to a high significance of localized knowledge spillovers, even though the globalization process is progressing further. Last, concerning different types of the German universities, it has been discovered that they highly differ regarding their knowledge, innovation and collaboration patterns. Hence, several policy recommendations are developed which shall help the German knowledge-based economy to be well prepared for future challenges.

Table of Contents

List of Figures

List of Tables

List of Abbreviations

ATP	Advanced Technology Program
BMBF	German Federal Ministry for Education and Research
BMWi	German Federal Ministry of Economic Affairs and Technology
CSV	Comma-Separated Values
DFG	German Research Community
EPO	European Patent Organisation
EU	European Union
ICT	Information and Communication Technologies
IGF	Industrial Joint Research Program
IPR	Intellectual Property Rights
KIT	Karlsruhe Institute of Technology
LMU	Ludwigs-Maximilian-University
Med	Medical University
MIT	Massachusetts Institute of Technology
Non-Med	Non-Medical University

Non-TU	Non-Technical University
NSI	National System of Innovation
OECD	Organization for Economic Cooperation and Development
OLS	Ordinary Least Squares
PATSTAT	Patent Statistical Database
PCT	Patent Cooperation Treaty
PPP	Public-Private-Partnership
R&D	Research and Development
RSI	Regional Systems of Innovation
SNA	Social Network Analysis
SQL	Structured Query Language
SSI	Sectoral Systems of Innovation
TFP	Total Factor Productivity
TSI	Technological Systems of Innovation
TU	Technical University
US	Unites States
USPTO	US Patent and Trademark Office

WIPO	World Intellectual Property Organization

1. Introduction

"Knowledge is power" Francis Bacon (1597)

As it is shown by the statement of Francis Bacon from the 16th century, it is not a new phenomenon that knowledge is regarded as one of the key resources to an economy in order to bring up new technologies and innovations. At that time, Francis Bacon still wrote about his ambition to bring the human being on a higher level of existence through the power of knowledge. However, it is not surprising that many scholars referred to Francis Bacon's statement, and further showed that the accumulation of human capital is the most strategic resource for regional economic development and competitiveness within our globalised world (Romer 1986, Lucas 1988, Grossman and Helpman 1991, Lundvall 1992, Becker 1994 and Romer 1996). Further, the relation between knowledge and innovation is self-evident as knowledge is widely seen as a crucial factor for innovation activity, so that innovation can be seen as the result of an interactive process of knowledge generation, diffusion and application. Thus, the expedient exploration of knowledge is essential for shaping successful innovations (Camagni 2001 and Katila and Ahuja 2002).

1.1. Universities in the Concept of Knowledge Generation and Innovation

A vast majority of nowadays literature confirms that in times of globalization universities have increasingly become involved in economic development and are often believed to play a key role in regional economic development as well as in gaining new technologies and innovations (Etzkowitz 1989, Etzkowitz and Leydesdorff 2000, Miner et al. 2002). Besides, the traditional university whose primary objective is research and teaching has been highly complemented by increasingly 'entrepreneurial university' which generates revenue and enhances its political viability through technology transfer and the commercial transfer of innovation. In this context, the famous cases of Stanford University and Massachusetts Institute of Technology (MIT) are often mentioned as they played crucial roles in the development of Silicon Valley and the greater Boston area (Etzkowitz 1989 and Etzkowitz and Leydesdorff 2000). Hence, the fully developed industrialized economies are undergoing important and fundamental economic and social changes, as, for example, pictured through substantial increases of the share of the total resources devoted to research and development (R&D) or changes in the educational achievements of the labour force. In this context, it is not surprising that the German academic landscape has become an ever more important issue as it plays an essential role regarding the creation of high potentials that are, in turn, responsible for developing, using and diffusing knowledge and technology. Being aware of the importance of new knowledge and innovation, it is further important to tackle the question how both can be developed and dispersed best. Already Lucas (1988) and Grossman and Helpman (1991) have shown that knowledge diffusion between actors within an institutional system is crucial for innovation and economic growth. Following Breschi and Lissoni (2001), those knowledge-based spillovers are not 'in the air', as they are the result of intended interaction between any social actors that simultaneously help to realise the innovation itself. Thus, knowledge generation and innovation is the result of a complex set of relationships among actors in a system, which can include enterprises, universities, research institutes and the government (OECD 1997).

1.2. Objectives

Following the introductory words, it is beyond question that the ability to create, access and use knowledge and technology has become a fundamental determinant of long-term development and competitiveness. Despite a growing importance of public research centers and private think-tanks, it is the universities who have increasingly become involved in economic development and are often believed to play a crucial role for regional economic growth rates. This PhD thesis exactly picks up this line of thought and explores the role of the German universities in a system of joint knowledge generation and innovation and applies a broad social network analysis (SNA) of publications and patents with a special focus on the spatial dimension. The aim of this work is to provide new insight into the behavioural patterns of the German universities regarding their knowledge generation, innovation and collaboration function. Thereby, it is of high interest how they have developed over the past ten years and to what extent academic knowledge transfer has become important especially to industry and of course to the broader research community. In this context, it is also asked whether the importance of the spatial factor has changed over time. Finally, this PhD thesis aims to provide appropriate policy recommendations which are closely tailored to the requirements of the German universities as well as to the needs of the whole German knowledge-based community in order to be able to tackle future challenges.

1.3. Basic Research Line and Structure

In order to achieve the objectives drawn above, the basic research line is set as follows. *First of all*, it is pointed to the highly increasing activity of the German universities regarding their publication and patenting behaviour as well as to their growing collaboration potential. *Second*, it is analysed whether the role of the German universities has changed from solely knowledge producers towards knowledge mediators, which leads to an increasing importance of universities as a central node for knowledge and innovation transfer. *Third*, this PhD thesis tackles the question whether geographic distance still plays an important role regarding close network collaborations as already discussed before. *Fourth*, three different groups[1] of German universities are explored and compared with each other regarding their knowledge generation, innovation and collaboration behaviour. Overall, the empirical findings are based on publications of the Scopus database and enclose several thousand publications for each university for a time period from 2000 until 2009. Besides, the EPO Worldwide Patent Statistical Database Version October 2010 (PATSTAT) is used, in order to measure innovation activities radiating from all German universities for the same time period.

However, in order to achieve a detailed overview regarding the role and behaviour of the German universities within their particular systems of knowledge generation, innovation and collaboration as described above, this PhD thesis utilizes the following structure:

[1] The terms group and type are used interchangeable within the course of this PhD thesis.

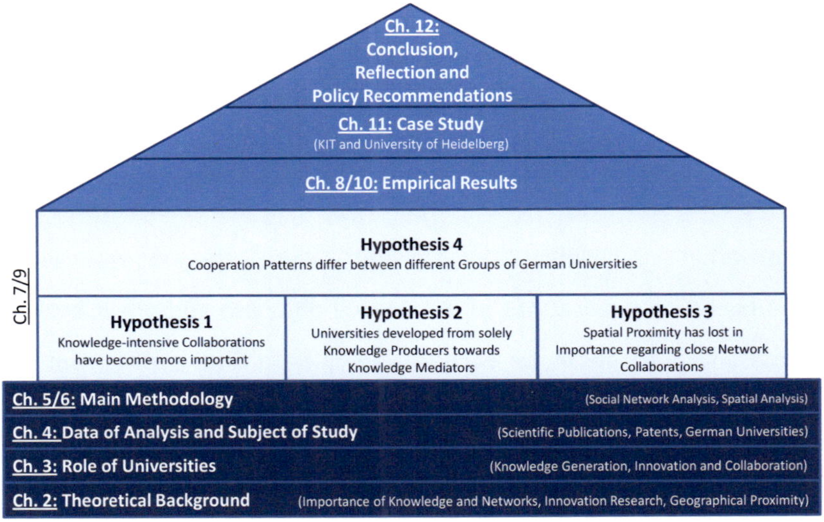

Figure 1: Structure of the PhD Thesis (own illustration).

As can be seen from the figure, this PhD thesis *starts* with the theoretical background and elaborates upon the concept of knowledge and innovation. Thereby, it offers a short definition of knowledge and shortly discusses the nature and concept of knowledge, as it is a driving force for innovation activity. Afterwards, the concept of innovation is illustrated through the illustration of different innovation systems, through several measures of innovation activity as well as through the relevance of innovations for an economy. Finally, the increasing importance of innovation networks is stressed followed by a short introduction of proximity patterns in times of globalization.

After elaborating upon the reasons why knowledge, innovation and collaboration are essential for economies that have experienced a fast expansion of knowledge-based industries and activities which basic raw material is simply new knowledge, *chapter three* is based upon the role of universities within knowledge and innovations networks. As already discussed, universities are seen as a source of knowledge intensive capital which is further beneficial for technological change, innovation and economic growth. This chapter illustrates an overview of university research in Germany, and simultaneously shows several support measures with regard to university interactions. It finally demonstrates the impact of university research as important driving force for regional economic development and competitiveness as well as several possible types of university interactions.

Chapter four illustrates the data of analysis as well as the subject of study. Thus, it presents a detailed introduction of both innovation indicators, namely scientific publications and patent applications that are used throughout the work. In this context, it also points to the scope of each data set, emphasizing that it can make use of around 250,000 papers where at least one German univeristy has been involved with over the past ten years. It finally introduces the German universities that are considered and offers a classification of the three different types of univeristies that are to be explored and compared with each other.

While *chapter five* is based upon the concept of the SNA, the *subsequent chapter* elaborates upon the concept of the spatial analysis. First of all, it is shown in how far the instrument of SNA is generally used and how it is applied in the context of scientific publications and patent applications. Thus, several centrality measures are introduced which help to identifiy the particular behaviour of the German universities regarding their knowledge, innovation and collaboration potential. Within the concept of the spatial analysis, it is shown how this PhD thesis deals with proximity patterns. In order to be able to provide appropriate answers on this topic, it is compulsive to be aware of all distances, measured in kilometres, which are to be covered between the German universities and their individual cooperation partners. Thereby, the ascertainment of the exact geographical position of each co-author has been calculated by the Haversine formula[2].

In order to give insight into role of the German universities in a system of joint knowledge generation and innovation, *chapter seven* illustrates all relevant hypotheses in this regard and simultaneously indicates the statistical tools that have been used to underline the results. The empirical results are further displayed in the *subsequent chapter*. Thereby, a broad overview of the overall publication and patenting activity of all German universities over the past ten years is firstly illustrated. It is shown how the role of the German universities has changed towards knowledge mediators, hence, indicating that

[2] See chapter six for detailed information on this topic.

cooperation patterns have become much more important over the past decade. In this context, the institutional distribution of the German university cooperation partners is also illustrated and points to the most famous university-university linkages, but also highlights the emerging collaborations between universities and enterprises regarding scientific publications. Those university-industry linkages are evident for the patent analysis and are also highlighted in this regard. A second cornerstone consists of an extensive spatial distribution measure which illustrates whether distance patterns still matter within the German university knowledge networks as it did years before.

Chapter nine introduces the hypotheses and methodology considering the different types of German universities, distinguishing between elite, medical and technical universities, while *chapter ten* further provides the empirical results in this regard. Here, it is shown how the different types of German universities behave regarding their individual knowledge, innovation and collaboration potential. Of course, proximity patterns in times of globalisation are again of high interest.

As significant differences have generally been discovered between the different types of German universities, *chapter eleven* presents a case study and explores the differences between the Karlsruhe Institute of Technology which is a technically oriented university and the University of Heidelberg which is medically oriented. These two universities have been selected as main differences have been discovered between technical and medical universities, and it is thus aimed to further confirm the empirical results of the previous chapters.

Finally, *chapter twelve* provides the final conclusion of this work with an overall reflection of the empirical results. Thereby, it offers policy recommendations and delivers simultaneously evidence for further research on this topic.

2. The Concept of Knowledge and Innovation

The increasing importance of technical advance and innovation regarding economic performance and development is a well-discussed and highly-accepted issue in the older macroeconomic theory (Schumpeter 1911, Solow 1956, Romer 1986, Lucas 1988 and Lundvall 1992, Grupp 1998). Thereby, knowledge is a crucial factor for innovation activity, so that innovation can be seen as the result of an interactive process of knowledge generation, diffusion and application (Camagni 2001 and Katila and Ahuja 2002). Van Hippel (1988) already stated that the resource knowledge is an essential factor for innovation research and practice, thus playing an important role in generating successful innovations.

As this PhD thesis deals with the increasing role of German universities regarding joint knowledge generation and innovation, this chapter now introduces the major concepts of knowledge and innovation. First of all, a short explanation of the term knowledge is given, as knowledge is a driving force for innovation activity. Further, in order to perceive a deeper understanding of the role of knowledge, the nature and concept of knowledge is illustrated. Afterwards, the concept of innovation research is pointed out. In this context, different innovation systems as well as several measures of innovation activity are illustrated. Further, the relevance of innovations for an economy is elaborated. Finally, the increasing importance of innovation networks is stressed followed by a short introduction of the importance of the spatial concentration of firms and institutions which lead to knowledge spillovers, thus, enhancing innovation activity, too.

2.1. The Importance of Knowledge

It is more than four centuries ago, when Francis Bacon (1561-1626) an English philosopher, statesman, scientist, jurist and author, already referred to the power of knowledge. In his Meditationes Sacrae (1597), he wrote about his ambition to bring the human being on a higher level of existence through the power of knowledge. Later on, many scholars referred to his expression and further showed that the accumulation of human capital is the most strategic resource for regional economic development and competitiveness within our globalised world (Romer 1986, Lucas 1988, Grossman and Helpman 1991 and Lundvall 1992). Besides, Von Hippel (1988) also stated that knowledge is an essential factor for innovation research and practice. Hence, it is not surprising that many scholars illustrated that the expedient exploration of knowledge is essential for shaping successful innovations (Katila and Ahuja 2002). But how can knowledge be defined? There is indeed no single definition of the term knowledge as its meaning goes often in line with the context it is used for. Referring to the Oxford dictionary (2012), knowledge is defined as “facts, information, and skills acquired through experience or education; the theoretical or practical understanding of a subject".

Plotkin (1994), for instance, sees knowledge as a kind of dynamic system from which information can be stored, processed and understood, and Blackler (1995) generalises that knowledge is above all an active process that is mediated, situated, provisional, pragmatic and contested (Howells 2002). Of course, there have been many attempts to identify and classify different types of knowledge. One of the first authors who tried to present a first distinction was Michael Polanyi (1958). In his early works, he distinguishes between explicit and tacit knowledge. The difference lies in the degree of formalisation and the requirement of presence in knowledge formation. Thereby, explicit knowledge includes expertise that is transmittable in formal and systematic language, thus, it does not require direct experience of the knowledge that is being acquired. On the other side, tacit knowledge cannot be communicated in any direct way, so that it concerns direct experience which, in turn, means that disembodied expertise is acquired via learning by doing or any other procedures (Cowan et al. 2000). But how can knowledge be best dispersed? As knowledge comes from individuals and not from the institution itself, it is arguable how to transfer this knowledge best into the institution's knowledge base, where it then can be managed and shared. Nonaka and Takeuchi (1995) have developed a simple model what they call the knowledge-creating company. For them, the interaction of tacit and explicit knowledge is the driving force for knowledge creation in any institution and provokes the four phases of knowledge conversion. First, externalisation stands for the conversion from tacit to explicit knowledge. This is, for example, possible through articulating tacit knowledge, hence, bringing it into an explicit form, such as a report or forum discussion. Second, the adaptation from tacit to tacit knowledge through sharing experiences and practice is called socialisation. This kind of knowledge conversion occurs, for example, in apprenticeships and at seminars and conferences. Third, Internalisation implies the conversion from explicit knowledge back to tacit knowledge. In this context, it is mainly about learning by doing and leads to operational-procedural knowledge. Last, dissemination means the adaptation from explicit to explicit knowledge, and appears when the owner of certain knowledge shares it with one another. This kind of conversion is the most common one and takes place through technologies such as computer-based training and groupware (Fischer 2006).

However, as it is common sense that knowledge is essential for innovation activity due to the fact that innovation is closely linked to the exchange and recombination of knowledge (Nonaka and Takeuchi 1995), the next subchapter now illustrates important details on innovation research.

2.2. Innovation Research

In literature, there are various definitions of the term innovation which have been evolving over time. Joseph A. Schumpeter is thereby often thought of as the first economist who draws special attention to this topic. So, it is not surprising that he is seen as the father-figure of innovation research. Hence, his early work from 1911 "The Theory of Economic Development" demonstrates the cornerstone of the innovation research era. There, Schumpeter distinguishes between economic growth and economic development. He states that pure economic growth occurs, if either the population or the resources of an economy increase. Apart from this, economic development stands for a "[...] fundamental change in the sphere of production [...]" (Schumpeter 1911). For him, an innovation must be something new, i.e. either a new product or a new production process, which must also have an economic effect[3]. In the 1930s, Schumpeter further defined five types of innovation:

- Introduction of a new product or a qualitative change in an existing product,
- process innovation new to an industry,
- the opening of a new market,
- development of new sources of supply for raw materials or other inputs, and

[3] Innovation is often classified as product and process innovation (see Schumpeter 1934 and Grupp 1997).

- changes in industrial organization (OECD 1997).

These different kinds of innovation appear spontaneously as well as discontinuously within economic affairs. First, they occur next to and compete with the old constructions until they become superior and displace the old ones from the market. In all, for Schumpeter, an innovation implies the phenomenal fact in economic history of a capitalistic economy as well as the basic fundament for changes in economic processes. The innovation process itself is classified by Schumpeter into three steps, namely into invention, innovation and diffusion. For him, the entrepreneur does not have to be necessarily the inventor of a new product or process. The entrepreneur translates the new idea into a business or other useful application and turns the invention into an innovation. Thus, Schumpeter already distinguishes between the pure idea (invention) and its market launch (innovation). But, he already indicates that not any invention must necessarily turn into an innovation. Besides, the third step is called diffusion which means the distribution of the innovation on the market, i.e. the process of diffusion is essential for an innovation to become well-known between different members in different social systems and implies the driving force for economic development (Schumpeter 1939).

Many authors now refer to Schumpeter's definition of innovation. Also the OSLO Manual which is produced by the OECD (1997) tries to set a kind of benchmark for innovation research. Today, the OECD identified four different types of innovation. The first one is called product innovation and can include either a new or an improved product[4] whose characteristics are significantly different from previous ones (Rogers 1998), i.e. significant improvements in technical specifications, components and materials, incorporated software, user friendliness or other functional characteristics are conducted; a product innovation within the education sector can be a new or significantly improved curriculum or a new educational software (OECD 2005). The second type of innovation (process innovation) is the adoption of new or significantly improved production methods, including methods of product delivery (Rogers 1998). This encompasses significant changes in techniques, equipment and/or software; a process innovation within the education sector can for example be a new or significantly improved pedagogy. Besides these two different possibilities of innovation types, additional focus is laid on marketing and organizational innovation. The former includes a new marketing method involving significant changes in product design or packaging, product placement, product promotion or pricing. Again, the education sector can for example imply a new way of pricing the education service or a new admission strategy. Last, the organizational innovation can be pictured through the introduction of a new organisational method in the firm's business practices, workplace organisation or external relations. A new organization of work between teachers, or organizational changes in the administrative area can be part of an organisational innovation within the education sector (OECD

[4] Product refers to goods and services.

2005). However, the basic message from the work of the OSLO Manual is that there is no consistent definition for innovation at all (Rogers 1998).

The following subchapters present different forms of innovation systems, as well as different measures of innovation activity, before illustrating the relationship between economic development and innovation activity.

2.2.1. Innovation Systems

In the late 1980s, a new conceptual approach appeared in the science, technology, and innovation studies which is called National System of Innovation (NSI). The NSI approach generally stresses that the flows of technology and information among people, enterprises and institutions are key to the innovative process. Thus, innovation is the result of a complex set of relationships among actors in a system, which includes enterprises, universities, research institutes and the government. To understand the NSI can help to identify important points for enhancing innovative performance and overall competitiveness as it can permit to find disparities within the system. Policies which seek to improve networking among the actors and institutions in the system are most valuable in this context (OECD 1997). Most authors agree that the framework itself comes from researchers like Freeman (1987), Lundvall

(1992), Nelson (1993), Patel and Pavitt (1997) and Edquist (1997) (Godin 2007 and Cooke et al. 1997). Freeman (1987), for example, puts the accent on the network of institutions in the public and private sectors whose activities and interactions accompany technical innovations. Lundvall (1992) defines NSI as "[...] the elements and relationships which interact in the production, diffusion and use of new and economically useful knowledge [...] and are either located within or rooted inside the borders of a nation state". For him the domestic interaction is most important and basically explains the existence of NSI. Nelson (1993) emphasises that NSI are a function of government policy at the national level, and Patel and Pavitt (1997) see NSI as national institutions that determine the rate and direction of technological learning in a nation (Niosi 2002). Last, for Edquist (1997), NSI include all important economic, social, political, organizational, institutional factors that influence the development, diffusion and use of innovations. Thus, the concept of an innovation system basically emphasises that the flow of knowledge, technology and information among private persons, enterprises and institutions is essential to an innovative process. Thereby, the interaction between the actors who are needed in order to turn an idea into a process, product or service on the market is indispensable.

The first author who used the expression NSI was Lundvall (1992) in his thought-provoking book "National Systems of Innovation. Towards a Theory of Innovation and Interactive Learning". The Idea itself goes even back to the 19th century where List (1841) is firstly associated with ideas concerning the concept of innovation systems. In his early work "The National System of Political Economy", he already records that every nation with its own language and literature, with its peculiar roots and history, with its special customs and traditions, laws and institutions is self dependent for its own development. Contrary to Adam Smith (1776) who advanced the view that the British capitalism was seminal for all other economies, List was convinced of the idea that proper economic development can be rather reached by considering the specific characteristics of economies than by imitating others (Freeman 1987).

Further, as innovation systems can be applied and adapted to different research questions, three further systems of innovation have been discussed over the past years, namely regional, sectoral, and technological systems of innovation. As the NSI is already explained in detail above, the following short explanations refer to regional systems of innovation (RSI), technological systems of innovation (TSI) and sectoral systems of innovation (SSI). *First*, the RSI is comparable with the national one, but includes only regions within countries or includes parts of different countries, whereas technologies and sectors are still neglected within this special system. RSI have been introduced by Cooke et al. (1997), Asheim and Isaksen (1997) and Cooke (2001), amongst others. For Cooke et al. (1997), for example, regions are '[...] territories smaller than their state possessing significant supra-local governance capacity and cohesiveness differentiating them from their state and other regions [...]'. *Second*, other economists rather highlighted TSI by centering on technology fields, i.e. the TSI explores a specific technology and is mostly not restricted by geographical or sectoral boundaries (Edquist 2001). *Third*, Nelson and Rosenberg (1993) gave some good reasons that support the sectoral conceptualisation (Christ 2007). Following their ideas, "[...] the system of institutions supporting technical innovation in one field, say pharmaceuticals, may have very little overlap with the system of institutions supporting in another field, say aircraft" (Nelson and Rosenberg 1993). Besides, Christ (2007) visualized the variety of systems of innovation as follows:

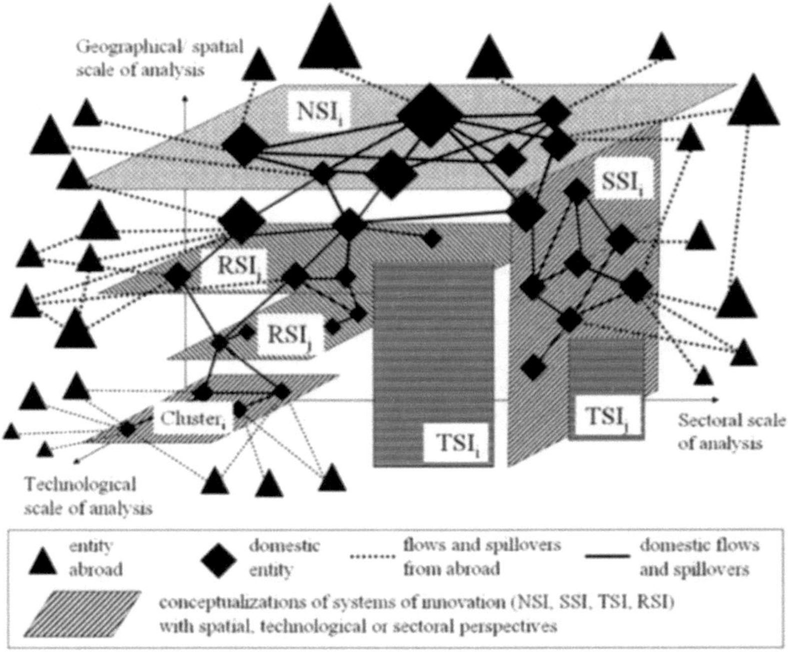

Figure 2: Varieties of the Innovation System (Christ 2007).

The above coordinate system now illustrates the interaction of the four different systems of innovation. The y-axis shows the sectoral scale of analysis, while the x-axis presents the spatial scale of analysis. Whereas the NSI and RSI refer to the geographical perspective, the innovation concept is also used for technological and sectoral perceptions as can be seen from the figure. Thus, academic literature illustrates some really good modifications and co-evolutions in reference to a more disaggregated level of analysis. Thereby, much literature is increasingly about a system of innovation that focuses on agglomeration and territorial innovation as Silicon Valley or Route 128 where sectoral specialization and causes of this local agglomeration overlap. Thus, it might be difficult to establish explicit distinctions between sectoral and local indications and perspectives. For this purpose, technological, organizational, institutional and economic changes within and between systems either on global, continental, national, or sub-national lines of argumentation have come to the fore. Additionally, technological systems can also be transnational and even global (Christ 2007). However, overall, this PhD thesis makes primarily use of the NSI, but also highly focussing on the regional perspective.

2.2.2. Measures of Innovation

It has widely been accepted that it is of high importance to be able to measure innovation, due to the fact that innovation is one of the main drivers of sustained economic growth, if not the single most important driver (Romer 1986, Lucas 1988 and Grossman and Helpman 1991). As innovation is a complex concept, it is not easy to suggest proper innovation indicators. However, in order to measure something which is not measureable at the first glance, special indicators have to be used which, at least, indicate a good trend of the development path of the certain object of investigation. Even though, there is no generally accepted indicator for innovation, Grupp (1998) delivers an overview of several innovation indicators. The following figure now shows the classification of three groups of innovation indicators and their typology:

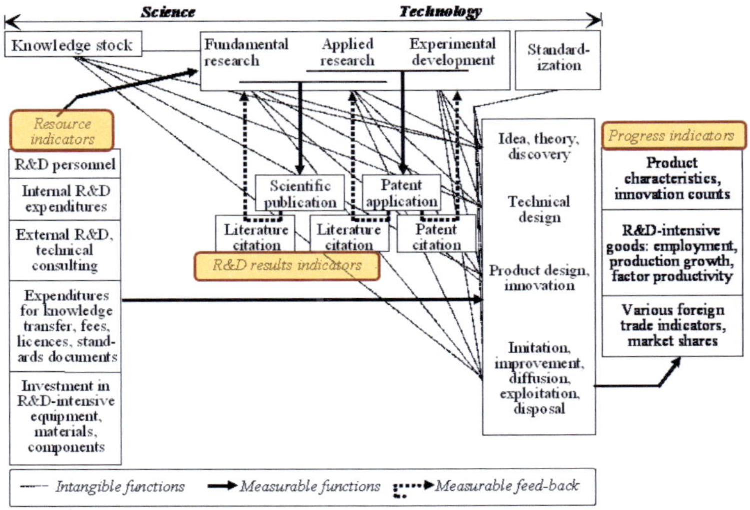

Figure 3: Overview of important Innovation Indicators and their Typology (Grupp 1998).

As can be seen from the figure, he separates innovation indicators into input (also resource indicators) and output (also R&D results indicators) indicators. A third group implies progress indicators which affect innovation on a micro and macro level of an economy. The resource indicators flow directly into the innovation process, whereas the R&D results indicators implicate the real effects of the process. The progress indicators primarily refer to the real impact of the innovation itself (Grupp 1998). In general, as this issue is a complex one, validity of any innovation indicators is restricted and interpretations should be done with caution (Acs et al. 2002 and Kleinknecht et al. 2002). Nevertheless, the use of any innovation indicators strongly increases over the last two decades (Lepori et al. 2008) as the access to data-bases became simplified and as the interest of policy makers, enterprises and the society regarding the usage of such indicators highly increased over the past years (Freeman and Soete 2009). But what do the three groups of different innovation indicators exactly imply?

The resource indicators stand at the beginning of the innovation process and encompass all measurable inflows into an innovation process. Due to this, they are also called input indicators. The overall input, thereby, often consists of several different inputs as R&D expenditure, R&D personnel and R&D-intensive equipment. Other inputs are governmental R&D subsidies, technical consulting, and all kind of expenditures and investments of knowledge transfer, such as fees, licenses, standards, as well as, material and components. In most cases, these indicators can be measured unambiguously in monetary units, even in different countries (Grupp 1998). Nevertheless, all resource indicators should be used with caution and demonstrate a rather restricted tool to measure innovation, as they only cover the inputs of the innovation process. Already Schumpeter (1939) stated that not all inventions must turn into an innovation, thus, also the results of the resource indicators must not necessarily lead to a market launch of a new product or process (Coombs et al. 1996 and Ejermo 2009).

In contrast, according to Grupp (1998), R&D results indicators try to measure the output of an innovation process, hence, implying any returns that result from R&D efforts. As can be seen from the above figure, the most commonly used indicators in this sense are scientific publications, patent applications and norms. Thereby, scientific publications are the outcome of scientific work and fundamental research and patent applications imply the outcome of applied science and experimental development. Norms are defined as a commonly accepted document which covers rules, guidelines or general standards which, in turn, encompasses codified knowledge of the state of the art (Konrad and Zloczysti 2010). As this PhD thesis uses scientific publications and patent applications to measure knowledge generation and innovation, both indicators are explained in detail in chapter four.

Last, progress indicators complete the set of innovation indicators. As already mentioned above, they do not refer to single R&D efforts but to the real impact of the innovation itself. They can further be divided into direct and indirect indicators. Direct progress indicators are, for example, innovation counts or the evaluation of product characteristics. But, it seems to be obvious that this kind of evaluation or the mere count of innovation implies problems, as it is indeed arduous and time consuming to carry out surveys which are engaged in such concerns. Long-run surveys are even more problematic as they are often not possible to conduct because of panel mortality and changes in the panel, such as insolvencies and mergers and acquisitions. Indirect progress indicators are production growth, factor productivity and a variety of trade and market share indicators. As trade numbers can be, for instance, extracted from federal ministries or annual reports of large multinational enterprises, they are easier to carry out compared to the direct progress indicators (Tran 2011). This PhD thesis makes use of the second group of innovation indicators, namely R&D results indicators, which are presented in detail in chapter four. Generally, it can be stated in this regard that knowledge creation, innovation and diffusion is very difficult to measure as there exist no conventional statistical variables.

2.2.3. Innovation and Economic Development

It is not a new phenomenon that economists appreciate the importance of technological progress in order to maintain sustainable economic growth rates. Adam Smith (1776) already referred in his book "An Inquiry into the Nature and Causes of the Wealth of Nations" to the advantages of technical advance through his famous description of productivity improvement in the making of pins. Later on, it was Schumpeter (1911) who pointed out that sustainable economic growth rates can be achieved through new technology and innovation. But, due to the limited mathematical capabilities applied in economics at this time, his work has not been displayed in a formalised way. Even though his work has not been considered for further developments of innovation theories for a long time, he has later on strongly influenced all further innovations theories. Elaborating upon the question of the relationship between innovation and economic growth, it is not surprising to go back to Solow's neoclassical growth model. Solow (1956) started to consider the influence of innovation by means of a classical production function[5]. First, one output (Y) and two inputs, namely labour (L) and capital (C), has been considered as demonstrated in the following equation (1):

$$Y = L^{\propto} * C^{1-\propto} * TFP \qquad (1)$$

In doing so, he was able to approximate the relevance of technical advance for economic growth by illustrating that the two input factors (L) and (C) of the Cobb-Douglas production function do not fully explain economic growth in the United States (US). Hence, as there must be another factor for this economic growth, he considered a third input factor, the so-called Total Factor Productivity (TFP), which now fully explained economic growth in the US.[6] Of course, also his traditional theory of economic growth does not yet clearly measure the role of human capital. Augmented theorizing on economic growth went beyond the limits of exogenous technological innovation and highlighted the importance of the accumulation of human capital as a determinant of

[5] Solow (1956) made use of the classical Cobb-Douglas production function.

[6] Note that exogenous growth theories comprise a whole class of theories, among which the model of Solow is only one among many.

economic growth (see Romer 1986, Lucas 1988 and Grossman and Helpman 1991), thereby, Lucas (1988) was one of the first researchers who considered human capital as an alternative to technological process to improve economic growth. Traditionally, education and learning by doing were considered as main sources of human capital, and, for that reason, many growth models have introduced these factors in their models. Following Romer (1996), countries need to understand the importance of technical advance, therefore, building up a knowledge-based economy to retain stable economic growth rates. Thus, it has widely been accepted that the ability to create, access and use knowledge and technology is becoming a fundamental determinant of long-term development and competitiveness. This PhD thesis exactly picks up this line of thought and explores the effect of the accumulation of human capital in the broad sense. Nevertheless, the entire Romer model[7] will not be introduced in the following as it is out of scope of this work.

However, as it is common sense that knowledge and the ability to absorb, create and exchange knowledge interdependently are essential for the generation of innovations, innovation and diffusion usually comes up as a result of collaboration activity within a net of individual and/or institutional connections. Thus, the following subsection now

[7] For a clear and detailed introduction of the model of endogenous technological change see Romer (1990).

introduces the importance of networks within knowledge generation and innovation.

2.3. The Role of Networks within the Process of Knowledge Generation and Innovation

Knowledge generation and innovation by a particular person or institution do not only depend on their own efforts but also on outside efforts. Hence, networking assists the individual or institution to get information and knowledge that they cannot generate internally. As a part of a network, the individual or institution can usually create greater opportunities for learning, hence, enabling to improve economic performance (Fischer 2006). The following subchapters now firstly present a short introduction of the analysis of networks and clusters. Then, the importance of innovation networks is stressed.

2.3.1. The Analysis of Networks

The analysis of networks has a long history and goes even back to the beginning of the 20th century, where Marshall (1907) concentrated on industries in Sheffield, Lancashire and other British regions, firstly using the term 'industrial districts' in order to describe a geographical district.

In this context, he considered the manufacturing industry where he observed groups of skilled labour and many small firms of similar characteristics. According to him, specific advantages could be associated with exactly these 'industrial districts' as, for example, specialization or the flow of knowledge, information and plenty of good ideas (Marshall 1907). However, the interest of network building highly increased not until the last two decades due to the fact that it has become a topical subject in industrial economic development and public policy (Sacchetti and Sugden 2003).

As there is no single definition for the term knowledge (see subchapter 2.1), there is also no agreement on the appropriate definition of networks. In the broad sense, networks are groups of interactive actors or organizations which are legally and financially independent from each other. Through this kind of informal cooperation, all participants wish to gain advantages from one another, perceiving themselves as partners and not as rivals. Due to the fact that the success of the whole network depends on each individual actor, it is evident that all involved persons follow similar goals. Hence, they usually behave cooperative and coordinate and match their activities forbearing (Hunt and Morgan 2000). Besides, Aldrich and Zimmer (1986) define networks as investments into cooperative ties between actors, in order to exchange and share knowledge and resources (Borch and Arthur 1995). For Thorelli (1988), networks are an interaction of nodes and lines, where each individual actor wants to enhance its position within the network.

According to Powell (1990), networks only exist, if all actors refrain from following their own individual interests to avoid that anyone else interests are jeopardized. Thus, all activities can be characterized as mutual and supportive for all actors likewise (Sacchetti and Sugden 2003).[8]

It is further important to distinguish between different types of networks. On the one hand, vertical networks take place along the production chain for particular products, whereas, on the other hand, horizontal networks occur between partners at the same level of the production process. Moreover, the shape of relationships may differ according to the relational structures between the independent actors involved, either internalized of externalized relationships. Referring to the externalized relationships, there are, on the one hand, formalized networks such as a joint venture which is formed by two or more partners which build up a separate company on shareholder basis. On the other hand, informal relationships, for example, between individual researchers who are located in different institutional settings, are highly trust-based as there is no contractual validation (Fischer 2006). This PhD thesis will focus on the latter, as it is about informal linkages between actors of different institutional settings, no matter if privately or publicly funded. Further, one important aspect within this PhD thesis implies the spatial dimension of network collaboration. Thus, the phenomenon of

[8] Scholars have, however, pointed to negative consequences of forming networks, too, as for example firms could get too focused on each other that they are not aware of other developments within the industry (Portes and Sensenbrenner 1993).

clusters should be also shortly mentioned in this context, as they are a special from of a network with a strong focus on the spatial aspect. Generally, clusters can be understood as networks of interconnected companies, specialized suppliers, service providers, firms in related industries and associated institutions, such as universities or research institutes, in a particular field that cooperate with but also compete against each other. Hence, according to Porter (2000), clusters do not only need local supplier chains to gain a competitive advantage but also close network collaborations. He further argues that competition rests on innovation and that close network collaboration with enterprises and other institutions is important, not only for efficiency, but also for the rate of improvement and innovation (Porter 2000). To sum up, network collaborations are able to create continuously innovations due to the fact that they concentrate knowledge and expertise (Simmie 2004), whereas clusters further focus on the importance of geographical proximity[9].

2.3.2. Innovation Networks

Innovation networks are a special form of a network, and consist of knowledge-intensive linkages between different actors. There are indeed many definitions of innovation networks. According to Koschatzky (2001), an innovation network can be understood as all

[9] See subchapter 2.4 for further information on geographical proximity.

possible organisational forms of different actors which contribute to the diffusion and exchange of information, knowledge and resources and simultaneously help to realise the innovation itself. Thus, innovation networks are social systems which concentrate on inventions, i.e. the development of an innovation and its market launch (Borchert et al. 2004). Another definition which is offered by Tijssen (1998) seeks to capture the most important features of the network mode. For him, an innovation network can be seen as "an evolving mutual dependency system based on resource relationships in which their systematic character is the outcome of interactions, processes, procedures and institutionalization. Activities within such a network involve the creation, combination, exchange, transformation, absorption, and exploration of resources within a wide range of formal and informal relationships".

Generally, much scientific work on economic development has focused on the increasing interest regarding innovation networks due to the fact that such networks facilitate sustained economic growth. Already Lucas (1988) and Grossman and Helpman (1991) have shown that knowledge diffusion between social actors within an institutional system is crucial for innovation and economic growth. Later on, Reid and Smith (2009) have stated that cross-institutional collaboration can be the catalyst for innovative economic development. Thus, innovation networks are seen as a kind of construction through which productive resources, social values and economic interests can freely circulate (Glückler 2007). Also

Breschi and Lissoni (2003) remarked that networks that include members from more than one country or institution allow for spreading knowledge freely among the various countries and institutions. For instance, many researchers have explored the relationship between networks and innovations by analyzing how these networks influence the frequency of patenting. They found out that there is a strongly positive relationship between network formation and innovation within diverse industries, and across industries. This positive relationship holds for network formation not only other enterprises but also universities. Further, within our knowledge-based economy, innovation networks facilitate the production of complex goods that are difficult to produce in their entirety within one single firm (Grodal 2004). Another stream of literature refers to advanced innovations which are said to draw on new scientific knowledge. This knowledge can be acquired through tight network collaborations with universities. Besides, incremental innovation are rather said to take place more in networks with partners from the business sectors (Tödtling et al. 2009). However, as knowledge diffusion between different social actors is critical for innovation and economic growth, it is not surprising that the literature on collaborative research networks and their impact on knowledge diffusion and innovation have increased greatly over the last years.

The following subchapter now finally introduces the phenomenon of geographical proximity in times of globalization, as this PhD thesis lays its special focus on the spatial dimension, too.

2.4. Geographical Proximity in Times of Globalisation

In an ever more globalised economy, it is arguable whether proximity still matters or not. Due to the growth of multinationals and global markets, economic theories often proclaim that 'geography is dead'. Also the rapid diffusion of the information and communication technologies (ICT) offers new opportunities for enterprises and institutions as it makes it possible to nearly completely neglect geographical proximity (Morgan 2004).

Before coming to the role of geographical proximity in times of globalisation, some concerns about the term proximity in the broad sense, and geographical proximity in the narrow sense should be made. A vast majority in the literature of various fields loosely refers to proximity as notions such as space, neighborhood, relationships and networks of professionals with recognized expertise and kinship (Torre and Rallet 2005). In the special field of economics, Rallet and Torre (2000) have presented a simple definition based on a distinction between two types of proximity, namely geographical and organized proximity[10]. Boschma (2005) goes even further and provides five dimensions of proximity, called cognitive, organizational, social, institutional and geographical proximity[11]. This PhD thesis refers to geographical proximity, which is, as its name already indicates, the

[10] See Rallet and Torre (2000) for further information on this distinction.
[11] See Boschma (2005) for further information on this distinction.

kilometric distance that separates two units in geographical space. Whereas the term unit could imply individuals, institutions or cities. The purpose of examining the distance of two or more entities is simple as it is for determining whether one is 'far from' or 'close to' any other unit (Torre and Rallet 2005). However, as this PhD thesis is about knowledge-intensive collaborations and innovation networks, it is always about actors who are connected by sharing the same reference space or knowledge. Here, the reference space consists of joint scientific publications and patent applications. Thus, the extent to which relations are shared in an institutional arrangement, either within or between institutions, is always present.

A key issue is now to determine whether the significance of geographical proximity on joint knowledge generation and innovation is still existent or decreased over time. A vast majority of the literature on economic geography suggests that the diffusion of knowledge clusters geographically, i.e. knowledge spillovers are rather found within a short distance. Jaffe et al. (1993) have shown this through patents that have been more likely cited by local patents than by patents that have been located farther away. According to Audretsch (1998), the diffusion of knowledge from the firm or university who create that knowledge to any other third-party is, on the one hand, essential to innovative activity, and tends, on the other hand, to be spatially restricted. Zucker et al. (2001), for example, have demonstrated that biotechnology firms are strongly influenced by the location of successful giants in academic research institutions. Lundvall (1992) has, further, argued that the importance of geography should differ by technology type. Thus, the importance of geographical proximity grows quickly for technologies that are undergoing incremental innovation and radical innovation. Other researchers show a geographic pattern in the context of European patent citations, as, for example, Maurseth and Verspagen (1999) have demonstrated in a study of over 100,000 patent citations between European regions that there is strong evidence of geographic clustering. Storper and Venables (2004) have stressed that the relevance of geographical proximity exists when there is uncertainty about the future and nature of a new product or process. Finally, Hamermesh and Oster (2002) have shown that the impact of information and communication technology on productivity or on knowledge diffusion across distance is not that great as expected. In contrast, the results of Arundel and Geuna (2004) have shown that firms interested in codified knowledge, e.g. in terms of patents or publications, are less likely to perceive geographic distance a barrier. Breschi and Lissoni (2003) expand the study of Jaffe et al. (1993) who has pointed to the importance of geographical proximity and found out that social proximity is more relevant for the degree of knowledge spillovers than geographical proximity (Cantner and Graf 2006). Besides, in times of globalization, Johnson and Lybecker (2012) have found that within the biotechnology sector, knowledge is more likely to diffuse over longer distances than it was true 20 years ago. Also Boschma (2005) provided a critical assessment on this topic. He has, generally, stressed that the importance of geographical proximity cannot be assessed in isolation[12] so that he has come to the conclusion that the phenomenon of geographical proximity is neither a necessary nor a sufficient aspect for knowledge-intensive collaboration or innovation to take place.[13]

This PhD thesis will now give a further insight into the phenomenon of geographical proximity in the context of knowledge generation and innovations and will show by means of scientific publications and patent applications if geographical proximity still matters as much as it did years ago.

[12] See Boschma (2005) for the classification of other possible forms of proximity that could matter in terms of interactive learning and innovation.

[13] As it is for collaboration networks in general, proximity may also have negative aspects on knowledge-intensive activity and innovation due to the problem of lock-in (Boschma 2005).

3. The Role of Universities within Knowledge and Innovation Networks

A vast majority of nowadays literature confirms that universities can be seen as a source of knowledge intensive capital which is further beneficial for technological change, innovation and economic growth (Jaffe 1989, Mansfield 1998 and Adams 2002). This chapter now firstly presents an overview of university research in Germany, and simultaneously shows support measures for university interaction. Afterwards, the impact of university research is illustrated, followed by an overview of possible types of university interactions.

3.1. University Research in Germany and Support Measures

The university itself is the oldest organisational form amongst academia and teaches sciences as a whole, in Latin 'universitas literarum'. Thus, universities are responsible for the management and advancement of science and art by means of research, teaching, studies, and advanced training. Thereby, it is the professors, institutes, hospitals and laboratories that help to accomplish their sovereign goal. Legally, a university is a public business operation which does not serve as pecuniary reward, but is responsible for welfare provisions. Thus, it operates on behalf of the state. The traditional university is, further, knowledge-oriented and does not consider the implementation and application of its research results, as it primarily offers higher education for scientific, political, and industrial executives. Hence, universities prepare young professionals for their occupational activity with knowledge and expertise within science and art (Zißler 2011). The research of German universities as well as of German universities of applied sciences is defined within the *Hochschulrahmengesetz (§ 22)* as follows: “Die Forschung in den Hochschulen dient der Gewinnung wissenschaftlicher Erkenntnisse sowie der wissenschaftlichen Grundlegung und Weiterentwicklung von Lehre und Studium. Gegenstand der Forschung in den Hochschulen können unter Berücksichtigung der Aufgabenstellung der Hochschule alle wissenschaftlichen Bereiche sowie die Anwendung wissenschaftlicher Erkenntnisse in der Praxis einschließlich der Folgen sein, die sich aus der Anwendung wissenschaftlicher Erkenntnisse ergeben können. Zur gegenseitigen Abstimmung von Forschungsvorhaben und Forschungsschwerpunkten und zur Planung und Durchführung gemeinsamer Forschungsvorhaben wirken die Hochschulen untereinander, mit anderen Forschungseinrichtungen und mit Einrichtungen der überregionalen Forschungsplanung und Forschungsförderung zusammen."

However, the evolvement of the German university as knowledge and innovation generator goes even back to the beginning of the 19th century, when the University of Berlin was founded (Schmoch 2003). It was Wilhelm von Humboldt[14], a German philosopher, who influenced decisively the organisation and orientation of the German university system. Idealists like him saw research at universities as an important element of teaching. At the very beginning, research at German universities was primarily focused on disciplines such as philosophy, mathematics, and humanities. Empirical research was not recognised and had to fight for its acceptance. However, at the end of the 19th century, research at German universities had already achieved world leadership in several disciplines such as medicine, chemistry, and physics; thus, many institutes with laboratories for natural sciences had been created. Simultaneously, due to the strong demand of German industry for skilled engineers, special polytechnical schools outside universities had been established. Later on, these special schools had even become higher a higher status, being now technical higher education schools *(Technische Hochschulen)*. Even at this early stage of the development of the German academic research system, there had already been university-industry relationships in form of, for example, consultancy arrangements from the university to the industry. Thus, the first forms of knowledge transfer appeared. However, universities and technical higher education schools were mainly focused on education, whereas the government established the first official research institutes in applied sciences. In 1911, for example, the Kaiser Wilhelm Society,

[14] Wilhelm von Humboldt was involved in the foundation of the University of Berlin, which is called Humboldt University of Berlin since 1949 (Humboldt Universität Berlin, Über die Universität, Geschichte, URL: http://www.hu-berlin.de/ueberblick, 04.09.2012).

the forerunner of the famous Max Planck Society, was founded. After World War II, further research institutes were founded such as Max Planck Society, Fraunhofer Society, and the National Research Centers (nowadays called Helmholtz Centers). The main evolution within the educational sector after World War II was the official acceptance of technical higher education schools as equivalent to universities, so that some of them even became "Technical Universities" or even normal universities after integrating some other nontechnical areas (Abramson et al. 1997). From this time, the reputation of application-oriented research could strongly catch up with the traditional basic research (Zißler 2011). But not until the 1970s, the German universities began to seriously regard themselves as important knowledge and innovation transmitters, and university-industry relationships, for example, finally grew by 25% between 1970 and 1980, and even by 44% during the 1980s (Abramson et al. 1997). In numbers, industrial funding of German universities rose from DM 110 Mio. in 1980 to DM 750 Mio. in 1997 (Schmoch 1999). Currently, in the year 2010, German universities spend € 12.6 Mio. on R&D. A very important programme to enhance higher education and research at German universities was the *Exzellenzinitiative* from 2005. At its beginning, the initiative implies three different lines of support. *First*, it is about the advancement of post-graduate schools in order to ensure the development of young German academics who find ideal post graduation conditions within a broad and interdisciplinary area of science. *Second*, clusters of excellent are highly supported to bundle research potential through networking activity at German universities. *Third*, it is about future prospects, i.e. universities as a whole are strongly promoted in order to strengthen them within international competition. Here, nine elite-universities have been chosen whose leading research and young academics shall be strongly supported. Overall, 39 graduate schools, 37 excellent cluster, and nine elite-universities have been supported with € 1.9 Billion since 2006. Then, in 2009, the German state and its federal states decided to expand the *Exzellenzinitiative* with a financial support of further € 2.5 Billion until 2017 in a second phase (EFI 2012). Thus, another 45 graduate schools and 43 clusters of excellence have been chosen for further financial support, as well as eleven elite-universities. The elite-universities now consist of seven former universities that had already been considered within the first phase and four new ones that could now persuade with their future prospects (BMBF 2012).

For a long time already, German universities could not be solely financed through public means anymore. Especially within the area of natural science, the project costs often exceed university budget, as the basic funding of the federal states cannot alone support nowadays development regarding the complex university projects within any area. Thus, university research is more often dependent from third-party funds, which sometimes even exceed funds provided by state government. Hence, it is not surprising that the importance of such externally funded research continuously increases over the past years. Thereby, the external money can come from the German state and its federal states, from public- and/or private-funded research institutes, and of course from industrial firms (Misera, 2010). In 2009, the German university budget has consisted of basic financing amounting to 73%, third-party funds amounting to 20%, and administration revenues of 7%. However, as already mentioned above, especially the importance of third-party financing rose during the past years, as € 1 basic financing covered € 0.14 third-party financing in 1995, and about 15 years later, € 1 basic fund already covered € 0.27 third-party financing (EFI 2012).

Of course, there are several different possibilities of financial support for the German universities. With regard to the German state, it is, for example, the Ministry for Education and Research (BMBF) as well as the Ministry of Economic Affairs and Technology (BMWi) that play the most important role in this regard. Thereby, the BMWi rather supported the industrial sector, as their programs are focused on the demand of small- and medium-sized firms. Their support measures are mostly found in the area of aeronautics, energy, and transport. The BMBF supports direct projects in other specific areas; currently, they are mainly engaged in new technologies, life sciences, and sustainability. On the other side, the federal states of Germany also aim at increasing their R&D expenses for collaborative innovation activities. In each federal state, the support measures consist of the increased formation of cluster, the enlarged foundation of innovative firms, and the better involvement of small- and medium-sized firms in innovation processes. Further, the German research community (DFG) generally fosters the

German universities in any scientific area. Here, the long-lasting collaboration between DFG and Degussa GmbH is to be stressed, as joint projects between university and industry researchers within the nanotechnology sector are highly supported. Further, the research association "Otto von Guericke" e.V. together with partners from industry, science, and state government supports different innovative projects; its portfolio ranges from basic funds until the market launch of new projects and processes. Thereby, the central point implies the industrial joint research program (IGF) which bridges the gap between basic funding and business application. Here, new technologies are generated for the entire industrial economy, whereas the firms accompany the whole research project in order to be able to adjust each step on their demands. Last, foundations play an important role regarding the support of university linkages and complement public funds reasonably. Here, the *Bayrische Forschungsstiftung* and the *Stiftung für Technologie, Innovation und Forschung Tühringen* especially foster joint projects between universities and small- and medium-sized firms (Wissenschaftsrat 2007).

3.2. The Impact of University Research

As already aforementioned, it has widely been accepted that the ability to create, access and use knowledge and technology is a fundamental determinant of long-term development and competitiveness. Hence, it is not surprising that in times of globalization universities have increasingly become involved in regional economic development and are often believed to play a key role in gaining new technologies and innovations (Miner et al. 2002, Etzkowitz 1989 and Etzkowitz and Leydesdorff 2000). Over the past three decades, the traditional university whose primary objective is research and teaching has been highly complemented by increasingly "entrepreneurial university" which generates revenue and enhances its political viability through technology transfer, the commercial transfer of innovation, the generation of spinoff companies, and direct engagement in regional development. In this context, the famous cases of Stanford University and MIT are often mentioned as they played crucial roles in the development of Silicon Valley and the greater Boston area (Etzkowitz 1989 and Etzkowitz and Leydesdorff 2000). This changing role of the university is surely a result of the shift from an older industrial economy to an emerging creative economy (Florida et al. 2006). Hence, the fully developed industrialized economies are undergoing important and fundamental economic and social changes, as, for example, pictured through substantial increases of the share of the total resources devoted to R&D or changes in the educational achievements of the labour force. These countries are also characterized by a fast expansion of knowledge-based industries and activities which basic raw material is simply new knowledge (Karlsson and Zhang 2000). Thus, it not surprising that the university, as a centre for research and technology generation, becomes increasingly essential for innovation and economic growth

(Florida et al. 2006). It is given and confirmed by various studies that universities have significant effects on corporate innovations as well as on regional economic development and are seen as a core element of a region's intellectual infrastructure (Lendel 2010). Jaffe (1989) has already discovered by the end of the 1980s that a greater number of patents are generated when business is located in close proximity to universities. Anselin, Vargas and Arcs (1997) have shown that the presence of university research tends to attract joint research labs. A vast majority of nowadays literature confirms that the use of academic knowledge is decisive for technological change, innovation and growth by means of new theoretical insights, techniques, and expertise of a kind that enterprises find difficult to provide themselves with (Jaffe 1989, Mansfield 1998, Cohen, Nelson and Walsh 2002). For Rosenberg and Nelson (1994), universities are highly important factors in the development of major innovations. Mansfield (1995), for example, has found that 10% of the innovations that have been explored could not have been developed without academic knowledge. In contrast, Berman (1990) explored that industry funding of university research can be associated with subsequent increases in industry R&D expenses. According to Becker (2003), existing studies have found out that joint research with universities increases the probability of firms to be engaged in the development of new products and technologies. Besides, Mueller (2006) has explored that the more firms draw from knowledge coming from universities, the more those regions see economic growth. In contrast, Mansfield and Lee (1996) illustrated that universities cited by firms tend to be the leading generators of new fundamental knowledge as MIT, Stanford, Harvard, and the like. Moreover, Kim et al. (2005) found that industry increased its research employment with experience on university research projects as well as with advanced university degrees. They also discovered that the percentage of patents assigned to firms that include inventors with university expertise increased substantially. Thus, the role of universities in the innovation process has changed and increased continuously over time due to the fact that the development of new products or technologies depends increasingly on the findings of university research (Martin and Nightingale 2000 and Tijssen 2002).

3.3. Types of University Interactions

The relationship between the university and the regional economy can simply consist of a transmitter-receiver system; i.e. the university is transmitting a signal that the regional economy must be able to absorb. Of course, if the regional economy does not function properly, it will not be effective to just increase the volume of the signal (Florida et al. 2006). Hence, both, the university and the regional economy must be equally developed, whereas the regions need to require an absorptive capacity to effetely absorb and use the scientific and technological results of the university (Cohen and Levinthal 1990). However, it is common sense that the innovation process itself is not a result of isolated agents (Monjon and Waelbroeck 2003). Powell (1990) has already stated that the sources of innovative capacity are mainly found between universities, research institutes and enterprises than inside them. Smith further argued in the mid 1990s that universities itself play three key roles within an innovation system. First, they are primarily engaged in scientific research, hence affecting the technological frontier of industry over the long run. Second, they produce knowledge to a certain extent which is directly applicable to industrial production (e.g. prototypes). Third, universities offer main inputs for industrial innovation processes in terms of human capital, either through the education of graduates, who become industry researchers or through personnel transfer from universities to enterprises (Schartinger et al. 2002). For Etzkowitz (1998), the interaction of universities and firms can be seen as follows: The product itself originates in the university but its development is done by a firm, i.e. a new product is accomplished through academic knowledge, whereas its improvement and market launch is done by a firm.

The reasons for firms to be active in any form of cooperation do not only lie in the fact that they want to share the costs and risks of research activities. Industrial firms also wish to have access to new markets and technologies as well as to be able to use complementary skills (Cantner and Graf 2006). Bishop et al. (2010) have also shown that firms benefit from interaction with universities in two ways. They gain from access to new ideas from fundamental research as well as from assistance with the market launch of new products. Moreover, according to Teece (1992), cooperation activity is especially necessary for competition on a level of high technological complexity. Moreover, Monjon and Waelbroeck (2003) have found that highly innovative firms benefit from official collaboration projects with universities. Lööf and Broström (2008) have explored positive impacts for large manufacturing firms, while Miozzo and Dewick (2004) have concentrated on the question of whether cooperation enhances firm performance in construction industry and found that there are positive effects from collaboration with universities in some European countries. Besides, in the case of US-firms, Darby et al. (2004) have examined that firms taking part in the Advanced Technology Program (ATP) of the Commerce Department patent more often when a university also participates.

Also, it is well accepted that collaboration activity is a significant and highly important channel regarding the diffusion of knowledge, as the number of partnerships among universities and enterprises testifies (Archibugi and Coco 2004). There are indeed many different forms of knowledge transfer as the following table demonstrates:

Possible University-Industry Interactions
Collaborative Research
Contract Research
Consulting
Informal Contacts
Joint Publications
Joint Patents
Conferences/Workshops
Exchange of Scientists
University Spin-offs
Provide High-Potentials
Diploma and PhD Theses
Provide and organise Seminars
industry-oriented Committee Work

Table 1: Possible University-Industry Interactions (according to Schmoch 2003).

Of course, there are plenty of possible university-industry interactions, but the above table covers a good variety of these interactions. Thereby, collaborative research refers to interaction between an industrial and an academic unit as the name implies. In Germany, such research is mainly found with programmes initiated by the BMBF as such research is highly supported since 1984. In the case of contract research, one single private enterprise most often announces a project and contract money out to one single academic unit which is in charge of resolving a specific technical problem. Consulting means that professors advice private enterprise, most often in the context of additional business. Besides, consulting frequently ends up with collaborative or contract research. Informal contacts imply informal meetings, telephone calls, etc., without any contractual arrangement. Publications are the traditional instrument of scientists to distribute knowledge. As industrial researcher also frequently read professional journals, publications are a substantial source of knowledge transfer. In the context of this PhD thesis, it is not only about reading professional journals, but it is about the increasing trend of joint publication between universities and enterprises (see chapter eight). More recently, joint patents obtain a more important role in the construct of university-industry interactions as can be also seen in chapter four and six of this PhD thesis. Further, conferences and workshops serve as good places to exchange knowledge, either of informal or formal nature. On the one hand, the presentations of research results can be used and on the other hand, conference breaks are useful opportunities to foster informal contacts. The exchange of scientific personal is deemed as especially effective as there is the possibility to transfer implicit knowledge. University spin-offs appear more often during the past twenty years, and are also an important source of university-industry interaction. Besides, the central function of a university is to educate high-potentials which can be then provided to any private enterprise. Hence, the provision of qualified graduates is also very substantial within the context of university-industry interaction. Diploma and PhD theses are often conducted in close contact to private enterprises. This can be realised either through contract research at the university or through the detachment of the graduate or postgraduate to the private enterprise. In addition, several academic institutes frequently offer advanced training courses for industrial researchers. Finally, many professors are members of industrial-oriented committees, e.g. in committees of technical trade associations (Schmoch 2003).

In order to limit the range of knowledge transfer channels, it is possible to draw on the work of Lööf and Broström (2004) who have introduced four main empirical indicators that show the growing relationships among universities and enterprises. *First*, they refer to industrial funding of university research and partnering projects (contract research), *second*, they mention patenting by universities (joint patents), *third*, they see start-up companies from universities, and *last*, they mention joint authorship of articles by university and industry research (joint publication). For this PhD thesis, two principal forms of knowledge transfer are taken, namely scientific publications and patent applications. Thus, chapter four provides an extensive illustration of the data of analysis.

4. Data of Analysis and Subject of Study

As this PhD thesis is about German universities and their increasing importance regarding knowledge generation, innovation and collaboration, scientific publications and patent applications are used to measure their invention and innovation potential. *Chapter two* has already shown that both indicators are proper R&D results indicators which measure the successful output of R&D efforts. Thus, scientific publications are now used to picture the invention activity of all German universities, whereas patent applications are further used in order to show their innovation potential. The following two subchapters now present a detailed introduction of both innovation indicators, before shortly introducing the German universities that are considered for analyses.

4.1. Scientific Publications as Innovation Indicator

Bibliography is traditionally the academic study of books as physical objects. Carter and Barker (2010) describe bibliography as a twofold scholarly discipline. *First*, they mention the organized listing of books and other works such as journal articles. Here, information on the author, the title, the publisher and place of publication as well as the date of publication amongst other can be found. *Second*, they bring up the systematic and detailed description of books as physical objects. In this context, it is about format and pagination statements. Generally, bibliometrics is a tool which helps to quantitatively analyze scientific literature (Oxford Dictionaries 2012). Of course, there exist different publication data-bases which can be used to analyze publication activity of certain authors and their linkages to others. The following two subchapters now firstly introduce the two most relevant data-bases, namely Scopus Elsevier and Web of Science, before presenting how the publication data from Scopus got prepared for all following analyses.

4.1.1. Scopus Elsevier versus Web of Science

The Scopus data-base, developed by Elsevier[15] in 2004, is an abstract and indexing data-base with full-text links. Its name comes from the bird hammerkop, in latin Scopus umbretta, which reportedly has excellent navigation skills. It took two years until the data-base was ready to extensively use, and during this time, 21 research institutions and more than 300 researchers and libarians helped to improve Scopus through verbal and behavioural feedbacks (Burnham 2006). Scopus covers almost 13.000 journals in the field of physical, health, life, and social

[15] Since Elsevier, one of the main international publishers of scientific journals, is the owner of Scopus, it established the independent and international Scopus Content Selection and Advisory Board in order to maintain an open and transparent content coverage policy. The members are from all scientific disciplines and geographical areas, whose interest is to access any relevant information regardless of the publishers (Hoogendoorn 2008).

sciences, whereof about 500 are open source (Falagas et al. 2008). The coverage period is from 1966 until today and the data-base gets updated daily. Besides, 60% of all titles are from countries other than the United States (Burnham 2006). The following figure now shows the basic search mode of Scopus.

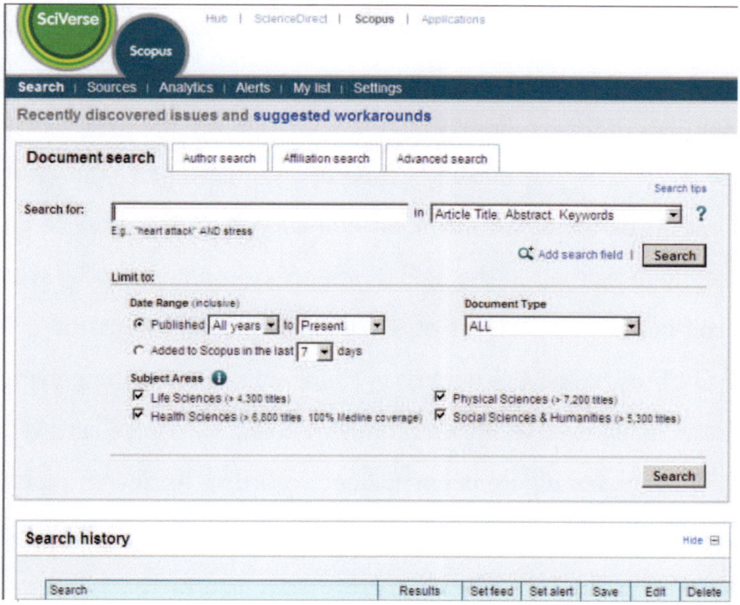

Figure 4: Basic Search Mode of Scopus (Scopus 2012).

As you can see from the figure, the basic search mode, for example, makes use of fill-in and drop-down boxes to search various fields. The search can be further limited to date, document type and subject area. Besides, author, affiliation, and advanced search modes exist which can be used if required (Burnham 2006). The results are generally displayed as a listing of 20 to 200 items per page which can be further saved to a list, exported, printed, or e-mailed. The results can also be refined by source title, author name, year of publication, document type and subject area. In this context, there are further fields that can be included within the output, such as citation information, bibliographical information, abstract and keywords, funding details, references and other information (Falagas et al. 2008).[16]

In contrast, Thomson Scientific which is one of the five operating divisions of The Thomson Corporation developed the famous bibliometric database Web of Science in 2004.[17] Web of Science covers almost 9.000 journals in the field of science, technology, social science, arts and humanities (Falagas et al. 2008). The coverage period is from 1900 until today and the data-base is updated weekly. The geographic coverage includes 80 countries (Burnham 2006). Of course, also Web of Science possesses different possibilities regarding its search modes. It has a quick search, an author finder, a cited reference search, and an advanced search. The following figure now shows the quick search mode of Web of Science.

[16] The following subchapter will present the search mode used for this PhD thesis.
[17] "Web of Science was created by Thomas Scientific to make citation indices (that E. Garfield assessed since the early 1960s) accessible via the internet" (Falagas 2008).

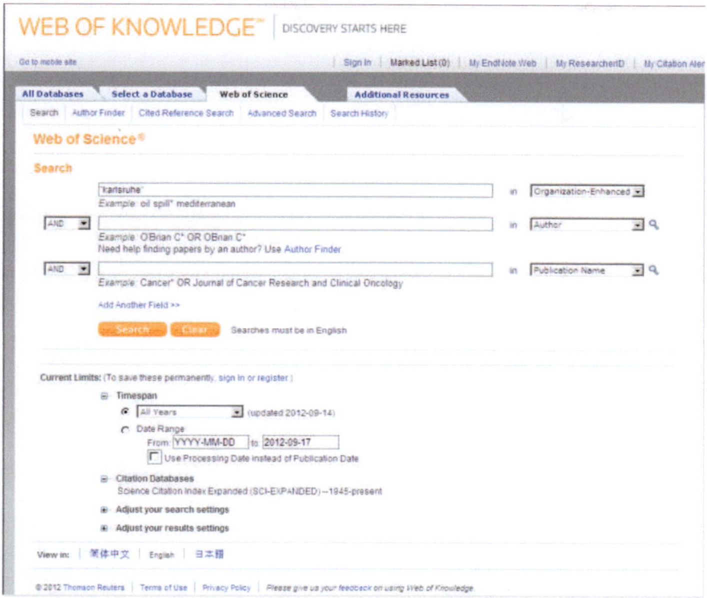

Figure 5: Quick Search Mode of Web of Science (Web of Knowledge 2012).

As it is for Scopus, this figure also shows for Web of Science that the quick search mode makes use of fill-in and drop-down boxes to search various fields. Besides, the search can be further limited to date. Limitations to document type and language can be made within the advanced search (Web of Knowledge 2012). However, the results are displayed as a listing of 10 to 50 items per page. The full title, author names, and source are provided. All related records can be further sorted by publication date, processing date, times cited, relevance, source title, conference title, and author name. Of cource, the results can be further analysed by author, country, or document type and it is possible to either e-mail all selected records or to print them (Falagas 2008).

Coming to a comparison of both data-bases, Falagas et al. (2008) found that overall Scopus has better features than Web of Science. They, for example, did a specific search on the word "brusellosis" and came to the conclusion that Scopus listed about 20% more articles referencing their search term in any given period compared to Web of Science. Thus, Scopus includes apparently a more expanded spectrum of journal articles than did Web of Science. On the oder hand, Web of Science provides better graphics within its citation analysis. Besides, Burnham (2006) concludes that it is easier to navigate Scopus, even for the novice user than it is for Web of Science. The ability to proper use the drop-down boxes allows for a comfortable searching within the intuitive search system. In contrast, Web of Science possesses the better coverage with its data-base going back to 1900 since 2005. However, it is obvious that both data-bases bear its own strenghts and weaknesses, so that they could be generally used interchangeable for all conducted analyses. The entire data preparation was extensive and not trivial at all; the decisive factors for Scopus were its much easier navigation and, of course, its free access.[18]

[18] The KIT is one of five German institutions which enjoys free access for Scopus.

4.1.2. Data Preparation with Scopus Elsevier

Again, as this PhD thesis is, amongst other things, about the role of German universities as knowledge generators, the publication data are taken to picture this development. Thus, all publications are filtered out from Scopus, where at least one German university has been involved with. Within the basic search mode of Scopus, the official name of all German universities has been filled in separately in the search field. In order to get the best possible matching in this regard, affiliation name could be further chosen within the drop down-boxes. This search strategy has been conducted for four years, namely 2000, 2003, 2006 and 2009. There were no further restrictions, as all document types as well as all subject areas have been considered. After choosing all document titles for one university and one time period, this data-set could be exported via comma-separated values (csv) file with the following chosen output criteria:

- Citation information, such as authors, document title and year, and
- bibliographical information, such as affiliations.

As the export data of Scopus has been not as expedient as expected, several additional Excel VBA macros had to be written. Thus, after exporting all data available for the 76 German universities from 1999 until 2010, the csv-files got further prepared until each author of a publication was assigned to its own publication-ID, country-code and year. They got further classified in being a German university (subject of study), any other university, a research institute or an enterprise.[19] The last step in this regard was the calculation of the weighting for each single author. In doing so, it was assured that the share of involvement was calculated exactly, i.e. if there have been four authors from the KIT, two from any other foreign university, and two from Daimler, the weighting for the KIT has been 0.5, and 0.25 for the foreign university, as well as for Daimler. This approach is especially important for institutional or geographical measures in order to avoid double or even multiple counts. Finally, in order to be able to conduct a detailed spatial analysis, each author got also assigned to its individual geographic coordinate. The detailed explanation of this procedure will be introduced in the context of the spatial analysis. The data set looks as follows:

[19] See appendix for the exact and detailed assignment of each group of authors.

pub_id	name	country	year	No of authors	weight	actors code	title	lon	lat
1000	RWTH	de	2000	2	1	11	Surgery of ab	6,08388611	50,7753472
1001	Uni Köln	de	2000	2	0,4	43	Anti-neoplas	6,96027778	50,9375306
1001	RWTH	de	2000	1	0,2	11	Anti-neoplas	6,08388611	50,7753472
1001	Department of Gyr	de	2000	2	0,4	1	Anti-neoplas	6,6572	50,9666
1002	RWTH	de	2000	3	0,75	11	Regulatory r	6,08388611	50,7753472
1002	KIT	de	2000	1	0,25	10	Regulatory r	8,38953378	49,0920474
1003	RWTH	de	2000	4	1	11	Non-redund	6,08388611	50,7753472
1004	RWTH	de	2000	3	1	11	Lipase-cataly	6,08388611	50,7753472
1005	RWTH	de	2000	2	0,66666667	11	An aphasia d	6,08388611	50,7753472
1005	Department of Aut	dk	2000	1	0,33333333	0	An aphasia d	12,49	55,76
1006	RWTH	de	2000	1	1	11	Pathogenesi	6,08388611	50,7753472
1007	Natl. Ctr. Nat. Sci. a	vn	2000	1	0,33333333	1	Differential nonhomogeneous models		
1007	RWTH	de	2000	2	0,66666667	11	Differential	6,08388611	50,7753472
1008	Klinik Aachen	de	2000	6	0,85714286	1	Changes in p	6,08777482	50,7771715
1008	RWTH	de	2000	1	0,14285714	11	Changes in p	6,08388611	50,7753472
1009	RWTH	de	2000	6	0,85714286	11	Potential of	6,08388611	50,7753472
1009	Department of Rad	no	2000	1	0,14285714	1	Potential of	10,75	59,91
1010	Department of Nu	de	2000	2	0,28571429	1	Diagnosis an	6,08777482	50,7771715

Table 2: Example of Data Preparation by Means of Publications (own illustration).

As can be seen from the table, each publication has got its own ID number, the name of each author, the country code, the year when the publication has been published, the number of authors that has been involved with the publication, the weight, the actors code, the title as well as its longitude and latitude. Having all this information, it is possible to conduct several detailed analyses concerning the aforementioned institutional and spatial perceptions.

4.2. Patent Data as Innovation Indicator

While the role of all German universities as knowledge generator is pictured through scientific publications, patent applications are used to illustrate the development path of all German universities as innovators.

Thus, in this regard, for all conducted analyses patent data are the basis. The following two subchapters now firstly introduce the phenomenon of patent statistics, before illustrating how the patent data got finally prepared.

4.2.1. Patent Statistics

A patent is a temporary monopoly, issued by an authorized governmental agency. It grants the right to exclude anyone else from the commercial production or use of a specific new device, apparatus, or process. This right is given to the inventor of this innovative device or process after an examination that pays attention to the novelty of the claimed item and its potential utility (Griliches 1990). Thereby, the guidelines for examination in the European Patent Organisation (EPO) claim that the invention needs to be a technological one, susceptible of industrial application, novel, and finally needs to involve an inventive step in order to be qualified for patenting. If the public institution finally grants a temporary monopoly to the inventor, he is enabled to fully dispose over the returns of the invention. Of course, the inventor can assign the right to use the patent to somebody else, usually to its employer, a corporation, or sell it or license for use by somebody else. Thus, patents provide a legal framework for the protection of an invention. The public itself sees the stock of public knowledge increased (Griliches 1990).

Patent statistics are a crucial tool for scientists, statisticians and policy makers interested in innovation and intellectual property rights (IPR), as they measure the successful output of R&D efforts (Carpenter and Narin 1983, Griliches 1984, Schmoch et al. 1988 and Grupp 1998). As innovation indicator, patents refer to technological innovations, mirroring a part of the existing technological knowledge stock of a sector, region, or economy (Frietsch et al. 2008). Further, while many distinct advantages regarding the usage of patents as innovation indicator have been discussed over the past years, Schmoch (1990) summarised these advantages as follows:

- Patents provide a broad documentation of nearly all fields of technology,
- they have a complete geographic coverage,
- the collection of exclusive technological information is possible,
- it is possible to collect the important global innovation in German and English,
- they have a simple retrieval due to the fine classification,
- patent data have a good availability due to existing data-bases,
- patents are rich in technological details,
- they have a strong relatedness to certain applications,

- they make it possible to collect bibliographic information, such as applicant[20], inventor[21], application years, etc.,
- they deliver up-to-date information, and
- statistical analyses based on patent data are less cost-intensive.

Generally, patent data make it possible to show innovation activities in time and through a geographical, technological, sectoral, and legal perspective (Tran 2011). The following subchapter now illustrates data preparation with PATSTAT.

4.2.2. Data Preparation with PATSTAT

This PhD thesis concentrates on patents which are filed at the EPO Worldwide Patent Statistical Data-Base Version October 2010 (PATSTAT) or went through the Patent Cooperation Treaty (PCT) filing process at the World Intellectual Property Organisation (WIPO). In doing so, it is assured that it is dealt with patents with a high-expected economic value (Frietsch and Jung 2008). In order to conduct all following analyses properly, the patent data had to be prepared in a certain manner. For this purpose, all German patents have been filtered out that have been

[20] The applicant is the holder and owner of the patent. They can be any kind of legal persons, such as a private person, an enterprise or an institute. In most cases, it is represented by an enterprise or any organization (Tran 2011).
[21] In contrast to the applicant, the inventor is the real human creator of an invention (Tran 2011).

filed at the EPO from 1999 until 2008. By means of Structured Query Language (SQL), the following information has been gathered:

- Application-ID,
- year,
- name of affiliation,
- nuts-code,
- country-code,
- application sequence number
- inventor sequence number.

After obtaining this data, each patent got further classified in either being from a German university (subject of study), any other university, a research institute, an enterprise or a private person. Here, one challenge was to filter out all German university patents, as in Germany the so called 'Hochschullehrerprivileg' prevailed until February 2002. This means that employees of universities (professors or scientific assistants) could freely dispose of their intellectual property rights, and thus appear as patent applicants (Meyer-Krahmer and Schmoch 1998). In order to filter out all university patent applications, it has been looked at the academic title to further check all patent applications with professors as applicants. Hence, it could have been determined whether the professor really worked at a university, and to which university he was really affiliated.[22] Besides, it is further concentrated on co-applicant

[22] This proceeding is also done by Meyer-Krahmer and Schmoch 1998.

networks, i.e. this PhD thesis focuses on networks of applicants, not on networks of inventors. Thereby, a connection between two actors is existent, if two applicants are on the same patent. Thus, the overall activity of German applicants is illustrated and can be compared to the changing role of the German universities as innovators. The prepared data set looks finally as follows:

appl_id	year	name	ctry	inv_seq_nr	appl_seq_nr	actors code	weight
16711203	1999	ForschungszentrumJüli	DE	0	1	1	0,25
16711203	1999	Aachen RWTH	DE	3	0	11	0,25
16711203	1999	Fröhling,Werner,Dr.	DE	2	0	3	0,25
16711203	1999	VonLensa,Werner,Dr.	DE	1	0	3	0,25
16723681	1999	Freiburg Uni	DE	0	1	16	0,2
16723681	1999	Leipzig Uni	DE	2	0	88	0,2
16723681	1999	Simon-Haarhaus,Birgit	DE	3	0	3	0,2
16723681	1999	Schöpf,Erwin,Prof.Dr.	DE	4	0	0	0,2
16723681	1999	Schempp,Christoph,Dr.	DE	1	0	3	0,2
16728592	1999	Ser.V.GmbH	DE	0	1	2	0,5
16728592	1999	München TUM	DE	1	0	13	0,5
16732937	1999	Pilarsky,Christian,Dr.	DE	0	4	3	0,1
16732937	1999	Specht,Thomas,Dr.	DE	0	3	3	0,1
16732937	1999	Jena Uni	DE	0	2	87	0,1
16732937	1999	Hinzmann,Bernd,Dr.	DE	0	1	3	0,1
16732937	1999	Hinzmann,Bernd	DE	2	0	3	0,1
16732937	1999	Dahl,Edgard	DE	5	0	3	0,1
16732937	1999	Specht,Thomas	DE	1	0	3	0,1
16732937	1999	Rosenthal,André	DE	6	0	3	0,1

Table 3: Example of Data Preparation by Means of Patents (own illustration).

Again, the table shows an excerpt of the data panel including the application-ID, the year when the patent has been filed, the name of each actor, the country code, the inventor and applicant number of each actor, the actor's code and the weight each actor has on the patent. A detailed description of the data application will be provided for all hypotheses within the following chapters, where the conception and methodology are introduced.

4.3. Subject of Study

This PhD thesis tackles the question how the German universities behave in a system of joint knowledge generation and innovation, and how they have developed over the past ten years. Thus, in a greater context, German universities are the subject of study. But as there are around 420 academic institutions in Germany, this PhD thesis focuses on approximately one fifth of them. But how have the academic institutions been chosen?

There are basically five different types of universities in Germany; the traditional university, the pedagogical university, the theological university, the art academy and the university of applied science (the German *Fachhochschule*[23]). The following table now presents an overview of the German academic landscape.

[23] The German *Fachhochschule* is a type of German institution of higher education that emerged from the traditional engineering schools and similar professional schools of other disciplines. It differs from the traditional university mainly through its more application or practical orientation and less research. They do not award doctoral degrees themselves. This and the rule to call professors with a professional career of at least three years outside the university system remain their major difference from traditional universities (BMBF 2004).

Overview of Germany's Academia			
	Winter Term	Winter Term	Winter Term
Types of Academia	2009/2010	2010/2011	2011/2012
Academia (overall)	409	415	421
Universities	104	106	108
Pedagogical Universities	6	6	6
Theological Universities	16	16	16
Art Academics	51	51	52
Universities of applied Sciences	232	236	239

Table 4: Overview of Germany's Academia (DESTATIS 2012).

The table shows all possible types of the German academic institutions from the winter terms 2009/2010, 2010/2011 and 2011/2012. In general, a slight increase of the number of the German academic institutions can be observed over the past few years. However, within the last winter term, Germany possessed 421 different academic institutions altogether, whereof 108 belonged to traditional universities, six to pedagogical universities, 16 to theological universities, 52 to art academies and 239 to universities of applied sciences (DESTATIS 2012).

As already aforementioned, this PhD thesis does not cover all 421 German universities due to a couple of reasons. *First*, as it is always about knowledge generation and innovation as well as about scientific collaboration, it would have not been very reasonable to examine the pedagogical, theological and art universities, especially with regard to their innovation behaviour. *Second*, data preparation, especially with regard to the publication data, was comprehensive and time-consuming so that it was impossible to prepare for each university all data in such a detailed manner. Hence, the German universities of applied sciences are not taken at all. Finally, off the 108 traditional German universities each university has been selected which is publicly funded, is able to reward doctorates, and possesses more than around 5,000 students[24]. Finally, there are now 76 German universities which represent the subject of study. As the analyses are also based on different types of German universities, they are also assigned to three different groups. Hence, each German university can be assigned to the groups of elite, technical and/or medical universities or in none of them.[25] The detailed illustration and classification of the German universities is shown within the appendix and will be further used for several statistical tests in order to identify possible differences regarding their knowledge generation, innovation and collaboration behaviour.

[24] Except of the Technical University of Clausthal (4,300), the University of Flensburg (4,700) and the University of Lübeck (3,400).

[25] It is of course possible to be in two of the three groups or even in each of them, as some few universities are both, medical and technical oriented and got further selected as elite university.

5. The Concept of Social Network Analysis

The SNA is a useful instrument for measuring the nature and extent of collaboration activity among economic development practitioners within a metropolitan area (Reid and Smith 2009). According to Tindall and Wellman (2001), a SNA implies the study of social structure and its effects, whereas the social structure is regarded as a social network which consists of a set of actors[26] and a set of relationships that connect the actors. Hence, the SNA concentrates on relationships between actors and explores the availability of resources and the exchange of resources between these actors. The resources can be of two different types, namely tangible or intangible resources. Tangible resources are, for example, goods, services, or money, whereas intangible resources consist of information, social support, or influence (Scott 1991). As this PhD thesis is about knowledge generation and innovation, it concentrates on intangible resources.

However, by means of SNA, it can generally be illustrated how countries, regions, institutions or individuals cooperate with each other, thus, demonstrating the development of the regional, national or international connectivity. So, the SNA method is designed to "[...] discover patterns of interaction between social actors in social networks" (Xu and Chen 2005). It implements this by revealing the

[26] The term actor can imply countries, regions, institutions or individuals and is used interchangeable in the course of this PhD thesis.

overall network structure, as well as that of subgroups within the network, then examining the patterns of interaction among these various groups. It is an interdisciplinary methodology developed mainly by sociologists and researchers in social psychology. Later on, the SNA has been further extended in collaboration with mathematics, statistics, and computing. Especially advances in computer technology, availability of computer databases and the emergence of several software packages like Ucinet[27], Pajek[28] or NetDraw[29] has allowed for the construction and analysis of scientific collaboration networks. All this made it attractive also to other disciplines like economics or industrial engineering as it now developed to a formal analyzing tool (Cantner and Graf 2006). Hence, the SNA has quickly developed over the last two decades as the fruitful combination of theoretical concepts with the numerous application possibilities has attracted many other research disciplines (Wassermann and Faust 1994).

The networks illustrated by the SNA are mostly described by a graph[30], consisting of nodes joined by lines, i.e. the SNA treats individuals as nodes and the relationship between individuals as linkages (Wasserman and Faust 1994). Thereby, graph theory does not consider the conventional representation of physical distance, but measures the

[27] For further information see http://www.analytictech.com/ucinet/, 21.10.2010.
[28] For further information see http://pajek.imfm.si/doku.php?id=start, 23.05.2008.
[29] For further information see http://www.analytictech.com/netdraw/netdraw.htm, 10.05.2011.
[30] See Wassermann and Faust (1994): Social Network Analysis; Cambridge University Press for further information on graph theory.

distance between nodes solely in terms of the number of lines which it is necessary to traverse in order to get from one node to another (Scott 1988). In the following, it is illustrated how a network can be constituted:

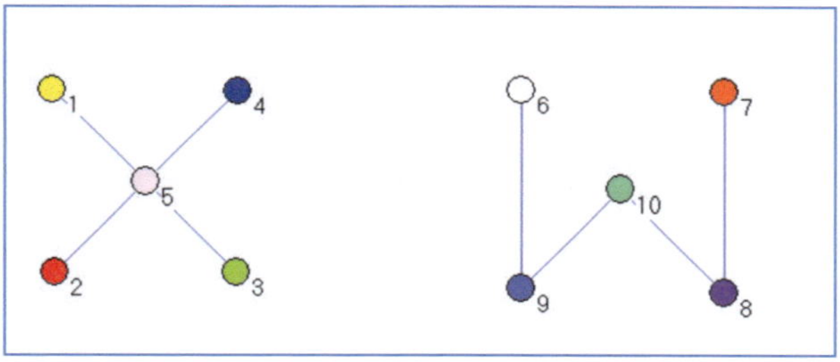

Figure 6: Star- and Line-Network (Nooy et al. 2005)

Figure 6 shows two possible forms of a network. On the left side, a so-called star network is pictured. Such a network is characterised by only one central node (node 5) which is linked to all other nodes (nodes 1 to 4). Thus, node 5 possesses four distinct linkages to other actors, whereas nodes 1, 2, 3 and 4 have just one distinct linkage to node 5. In this context, it is feasible to determine which node the most centralised one is, namely node 5. On the right side, a so-called line-graph is illustrated. In this case, nodes 8, 9 and 10 have two distinct linkages each, whereas nodes 6 and 7 possess only one linkage each. Hence, it is now much more difficult to find out which node is the most centralised one. Therefore, network characteristics have to be used in order to find out which actor might be the most linked and centralised one within a network (Nooy et al., 2005). Thus, centrality measures help to explore, if an actor who is highly centralised is also responsible for the support of innovations. Thereby, centrality can be measured by means of different methods. There are basically three applied types of centrality, namely degree centrality, betweenness centrality, and closeness centrality.

On the one side, the degree centrality of an actor is important as this measure implies the simplest possibility to determine the actors' centrality. Here, it is defined that central actors must be the most active in the sense that they have the most linkages to other actors in the network. Degree centrality is expressed as follows:

$$C_D(n_i) = d(n_i)/(g-1)$$

$C_D(n_i)$ - Degree-centrality

$d(n_i)$ - Number of linkages (degree)

g - Number of actors of the network (size of the network).

The higher the degree-centrality the more active is the actor within the network and can use its position to influence others agents or to get more information. Degree centrality can be seen as a measurement of communication activity of an agent. The following network shows the actor with the highest value of degree centrality:

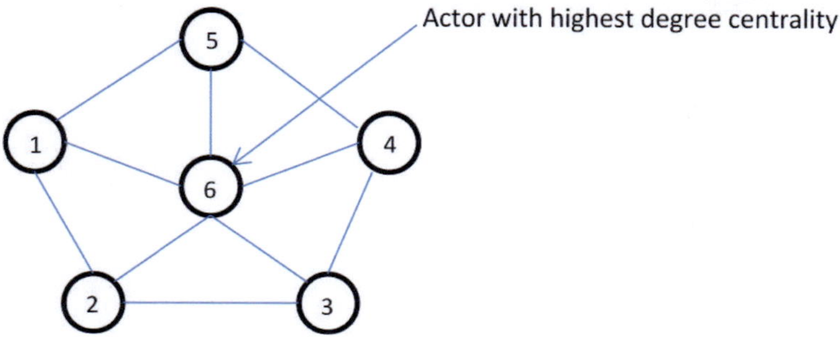

Figure 7: A social Network – highest Degree Centrality (own illustration).

Second, the centrality of an actor is based on closeness or distance, focusing on how close an actor is to all other actors in the set of actors. Thus, if an actor can quickly interact with all other actors, it possesses a high value of closeness centrality and is not reliant on any other actor for the relaying of any information. The concept of closeness centrality is available only for strongly connected graphs[31]. The value of closeness centrality is calculated as follows:

$$C_c(n_i) = \frac{g-1}{\sum_{j=1}^{g} d(n_i, n_j)}$$

where actor closeness centrality is the inverse of the sum of geodesic distances from actor *i* to the *g-1* other actors, and can be normalized by *g-1* (Wassermann and Faust, 1994). The higher the value of closeness centrality the less an actor has to rely on the transmission of any

[31] Connected graphs are graphs without isolated nodes.

information from any other actor. The highest value of closeness centrality within a network can be pictured as follows:

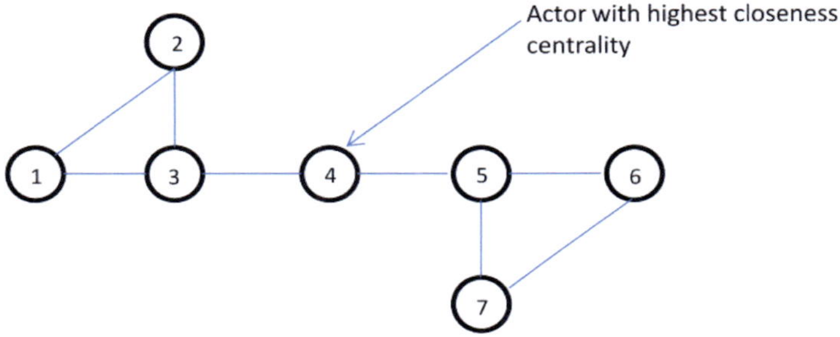

Figure 8: A social network – highest Closeness Centrality (own illustration).

While degree and closeness centrality always regard double relationships of the considered actor[32], the value of betweeness centrality considers three actors. It measures the extent to which an actor is needed as a link in the chains of contacts, facilitating the spread of information through the network. It counts how often one actor lies on the shortest path between two other actors, hence, taking into account the connectivity of the node's neighbours, giving a higher value for nodes which bridge clusters (see Nooy et al., 2005). The value of betweenness centrality is defined as follows:

[32] The difference is that degree centrality only considers direct relationships and closeness centrality also indirect linkages.

$$C_B(n_i) = \sum_{j \neq n \neq k} g_{jk}(n_i) / g_{jk}$$

$g_{jk}(n_i)$ -Number of shortest path between two nodes j and k (geodesics) where node n_i is involved.

g_{jk} - Number of shortest paths between two nodes j and k

$C_b(n_i)$ - Betweenness centrality

The higher the value of betweenness centrality the more important is the actor within the network, i.e. the actor possesses a strong transmitter function within the network so that he is strongly needed for the transmission of information. The following figure shows two actors within a network which possess both the highest value of betweenness centrality:

Figure 9: A social network – highest Betweenness Centrality (own illustration).

Again, as it is intended to demonstrate how strong all German universities are generally linked to other actors within the knowledge and innovation networks, the concepts of degree and betweenness centrality are used for further analyses within this PhD thesis. As already mentioned above, the emergence of several software packages like Ucinet, Pajek or NetDraw has allowed for the construction and analysis of scientific collaboration networks which contain huge mounds of data. Here, the software package Pajek is used in order to draw networks and to calculate above mentioned centrality measures. However, before doing this, the publication and patent data had to be prepared in a special manner. First of all, they had to be set up as follows:

Patent Data					
Application-ID	Affiliation of Applicant	Country-Code	Application Sequence No.	Inventor Sequence No.	Year
1000000	KIT	DE	1	0	2008
1000000	University of Tc	CA	2	0	2008
1000001	KIT	DE	1	0	2009
etc.					

Table 5: Example of Patent Data Set-up for Data Preparation with Java (own illustration).

Publication Data					
Application-ID	Affiliation of Applicant	Country-Code	Application Sequence No.	Inventor Sequence No.	Year
1000000	KIT	DE	-	-	2008
1000000	University of Tc	CA	-	-	2008
1000001	KIT	DE	-	-	2009
etc.					

Table 6: Example of Publication Data Set-Up for Data Preparation with Java (own illustration).[33]

A Java-written program further prepared both data sets in such a manner that they could be used for drawing networks and calculating degree and betweenness centrality. Thereby, the linkages of each actor are weighted, i.e. each linkage of an actor to a patent or publication is divided by the sum of all linkages that appear on the patent or publication. In doing so, the sum of all linkages for one patent or publication is always 1. The final value of an actor then results from the sum of all its weighted linkages that appears on any patent or publication. The following example clarifies this approach by means of publications.[34]

---

[33] As can be seen from the table, the columns application sequence number and inventor sequence number are only needed for the patent data, as in this context, it is possible to explore co-applicant or co-inventor networks. For the preparation of the publication data, both columns are not required as it is always about co-authorship, no other classification could be made in this regard.

[34] The chosen example is according to the example illustrated in the dissertation of Bertram (2011).

Publication	1	1	2	2	2	3	3	4	4
Author	A	B	A	B	C	B	D	C	D

Table 7: An Example of a Social Network – Part 1 (own illustration).

The network of this example consists of four actors (A, B, C, D) who have the following weighted linkages:

Author	A	B	C	D
Linkages	0,83	1,33	0,83	1,00

Table 8: An Example of a Social Network – Part 2 (own illustration).

The network of this example looks as follows and shows all corresponding linkages of actor A, B, C and D, whereas actor A and actor D have no linkage to each other.

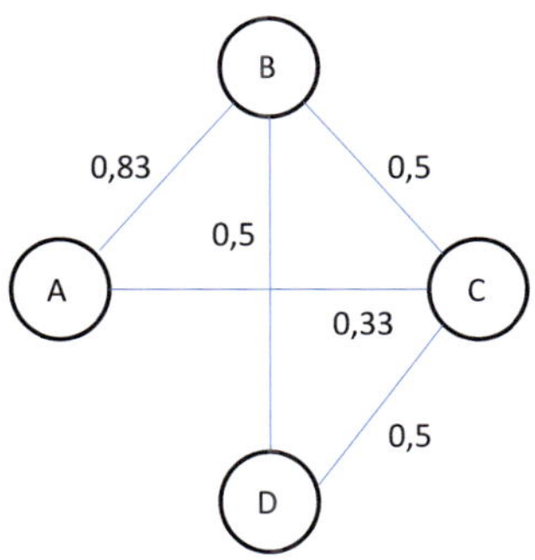

Figure 10: An Example of a social Network – Part 3 (own illustration).

After having presented how the networks of publications and patents are constituted, the following chapter now introduces the concept of the spatial analysis that has been applied in the course of this PhD thesis.

6. The Concept of the Spatial Analysis

As already discussed in subchapter 2.4, it is arguable whether geographical proximity still matters in an ever more globalised economy. The growth of multinationals and global markets as well as the rapid diffusion of the ICT may lead to the conclusion that geography matters much less than did years before. There are many new opportunities for enterprises and institutions which make it possible to nearly completely neglect geographical proximity. In order to provide another or even new input on the topic of joint knowledge generation, the used publication data firstly need to get further prepared. Hence, in order to be able to provide appropriate answers on the topic of geographical proximity, it is necessary to be aware of all distances, measured in kilometres, which are to be covered between the German universities and their individual cooperation partners. Thereby, the ascertainment of the exact geographical position of each co-author has been conducted as follows.

First of all, the detailed information for each German university and each German university co-author on its address could be used, as it was possible to filter out each individual postal code. By means of another macro, the postal codes could be further assigned to their geographical coordinates, namely its latitude and longitude.[35] If some

[35] A listing is existent in which each German post-code appears with its corresponding geographical coordinate, so that it was possible to develop a macro which could search for the post-code, simultaneously recording its latitude and longitude in a new column.

post-codes were missing, another search strategy had to be chosen. Thus, frequently occurring cities need to be firstly assigned to their individual post-code, after assigning them to their individual geographical coordinates. Besides, as all German universities are considered, and as some of them are located close to the national border, not only German co-authors but also all co-authors from adjacent countries who are located within a particular radius are considered in this regard as well. As there was no listing available which covers all possible foreign post-codes and their geographical coordinates, frequently occurring cities of each foreign adjacent country were again firstly chosen. Afterwards, they got assigned to their individual geographical coordinates, too. Of course, this procedure was time-consuming, but, as it is aimed to find out whether proximity still matters, a geographical radius has been chosen that narrows down the actors that have to be assigned to their individual geographical coordinates. Finally, a radius of 1,000 kilometer has been adopted due to two reasons; first of all, it can be said that the farthest distance that has to be covered between any two German universities is about 1,000 kilometer (e.g. from Flensburg to Munich or from Greifswald to Freiburg). Secondly, it is assumed that any collaboration that is farer away than 1,000 km is not considered as a regional one anymore; thus, distance of more than 1,000 km is not dependent anymore on the cooperation activity of the German universities.[36,37]

[36] See KIT – Impulsgeber für Karlsruhe und die TechnologieRegion, Kowalski und

Finally, as each co-author as well as each German university got its individual latitude and longitude, all distances could be calculated and assigned by means of a further self-written macro[38]. The calculation itself is done by the Haversine theorem[39] (Gellert et al. 1989):

$$d = 2r \arcsin\left(\sqrt{sin^2(\emptyset_2 - \emptyset_1) + \cos(\emptyset_1)cos(\emptyset_2)sin^2\left(\frac{\lambda_2 - \lambda_1}{2}\right)}\right)$$

d = distance between the two points.

r = earth's radius.

Φ_1 = latitude of point 1.

Φ_2 = latitude of point 2.

λ_1 = longitude of point 1.

λ_2 = longitude of point 2.

Schaffer (2012).

[37] Of course, there is a lot of university interaction on longer distances which will be considered for further analyses and is displayed in the following chapters.

[38] See appendix for further information on this macro.

[39] Of course, there are empirical approaches in the area of transportation modeling which consider road networks, railway networks or the air space in order to measure distances between any two actors using travel time. This PhD thesis has used the Haversine theorem which measures distances in km and not in hours. Using a complex transportation model would not have been productive for the conducted analyses. A transportation model which considers not only the three possibilities of using roads, railways or the air space but also high-stressed traffic networks would definitely gain too much weight in this regard.

Thus, the set of publication data can be separated into two parts. On the one hand, all cooperation partners within the 1,000 km radius can be taken in order to show first results regarding proximity patterns. Second, the geographical distribution of the German university co-authors within the 1,000 km radius has been taken for a subsequent cluster analysis. Generally, cluster analysis groups sets of any objects in such a way that those who are in the same group are more similar to each other than to those in other groups. In this context, by means of SPSS statistics[40,41] each co-author which resides in the above mentioned 1,000 km radius could be classified as either being a regional partner or a supra-regional one. The analysis has been conducted for four time periods and has delivered the following cut-off points for the data set with all co-authors that are within the mentioned radius:

Results of the Cluster Analysis	
	Cut-Off Points (km)
2000	508
2003	427
2006	537
2009	402

Table 9: Results of the Cluster Analysis, 2000-2009 (own illustration).

[40] By means of SPSS a kind of cluster analysis has been conducted which has grouped all German university co-authors according to its particular distances to any German university that has been subject of study. The SPSS TwoStep Clustering Component is a scalable cluster analysis algorithm designed to handle very large datasets. Capable of handling both continuous and categorical variables and attributes, it requires only one data pass in the procedure. In this context, the BIRCH algorithm has been used and the Bayesian Information Criterion.

[41] See Bellgardt (2004) for further information on applying SPSS.

According to the table, in 2000, all co-authors that have been located in any German university within a radius of 508 km are recorded as regionally located, for 2003 any that were located within a radius of 427 km, for 2006, the cut-off point was at 537 km and finally for 2009, it has again decreased to 402 km.[42] Thus, by means of the cluster analysis, it is secondly looked at the overall spatial distribution of all German university co-authors either being regionally located or supra-regionally[43].

Up to this point, it is known where about the German university co-authors are located, either regional or supra-regional based on the results of the cluster analysis; thus, there are up to now two decisions to make in this regard. Therefore, a second step is based upon the geographical distribution of the German university co-authors depending on where they are coming from; hence, it is a country-based analysis. In doing so, it is ensured to also pay attention on different groups of countries. Due to the fact that the German university co-authors come from around 140 different countries, five different groups of countries have been developed in this regard. They are as follows:

- EU15, including Belgium, Denmark, Finland, France, Germany, Greece, Ireland, Italy, Luxembourg, Netherland, Austria,

[42] The average cut-off point is approximately 468 km and will be used for further analyses.

[43] Supra-regional refers to all German university co-authors that are beyond the average cut-off point, also including those co-authors that are beyond the 1,000 km radius.

Portugal, Sweden, Spain and United Kingdom (all calculations without Germany plus Switzerland and Norway).

- EU12, including Bulgaria, Estonia, Lithuania, Latvia, Malta, Poland, Romania, Slovakia, Slovenia, Czech Republic, Hungary and Cyprus.
- North America, including the three largest partners, namely the United States (US), Canada and Mexico.
- BRIC, including Brazil, Russia, India and China, and
- JANZ, including Japan, Australia and New Zealand.

The hypotheses and the empirical results for both steps are illustrated in the following chapters according to the spatial analysis.

7. Hypotheses and Methodology regarding the Analysis of the German Universities

The basic concept of this work is to picture the role of all German universities regarding joint knowledge generation and innovation. Thus, in order to give insight into this construct, this chapter now illustrates all relevant hypotheses of the PhD thesis and simultaneously indicates the statistical tools that are used to underpin the empirical results. Thereby, this chapter is divided into two parts. First of all, a broad overview of the overall publication and patenting activity of all German universities over the past ten years is illustrated. Thus, it illustrates the German universities as knowledge generators by means of scientific publications, and secondly, it illustrates the role of the German universities in innovation activities through patent applications. In this context, the institutional distribution of the German university cooperation partners is also shown and points to the most important university-university linkages, but also highlights the emerging collaborations between universities and enterprises concerning the scientific publications. Regarding the patent applications, the highly increasing co-applicant networks with enterprises are especially highlighted. Thereby, it makes use of the SNA in order to identify which German universities are nowadays highly involved in close network collaborations and points to those that have developed best over the past ten years in this regard.

A second cornerstone consists of an extensive spatial distribution measure which illustrates whether distance patterns still matter within the German university knowledge networks as it did years before. First of all, it is shown to what extent proximity still matters by considering all co-authors that are within the 1,000 km corridor. Second, by means of the cluster analysis, all German university co-authors are considered, illustrating how all German university co-authors are spatially distributed, either being regional or supra-regional located. Finally, the spatial analysis makes use of the five established groups of countries, in order to geographically show how the co-authors of the German universities are spread worldwide. As it is done for the first part, this one also highlights the institutional distribution of the German university cooperation partners and points again to the four different university interactions, namely to all linkages to universities, research institutes, enterprises and to themselves, of course with regard to the spatial dimension.[44]

7.1. Knowledge Generation, Innovation and Collaboration

This subchapter now illustrates which hypotheses are to be explored and answered in the course of this PhD thesis with regard to the

[44] This broad spatial analysis is only based upon publication data as the data set of the patent applications is still too low to identify specific behavioural patterns in this regard.

knowledge generation, innovation and collaboration potential of the German universities in general.

First of all, it is about the publication and patenting activity of the German universities which has highly increased over the past ten years. In addition, it is not only the number of publications and patents that has enjoyed a great increase, but also collaborations for knowledge and innovation have become a lot more important. As mentioned before, nowadays, most countries are faced with a fast expansion of knowledge-based industries and activities whose basic raw material is simply new knowledge (Karlsson and Zhang 2009). Regarding the increase of scientific publications, Godin and Gingras (2000) have illustrated for Canada that the presence of universities in scientific papers has increased from 75% in 1980 to 81.9% in 1995. Katz and Hicks (1997) have shown that in the UK the percentage papers with at least one university in it have risen from 59.2% in 1981 to 64.3% in 1994. Further, with regard to the rise of patent applications by universities, a vast majority of nowadays literature confirms that the use of academic knowledge is decisive for technological change, innovation and growth by means of new theoretical insights, techniques, and expertise (Mansfield 1998, Cohen, Nelson and Walsh 2002). Besides, Rosenberg and Nelson (1994) have shown that universities are highly important factors in the development of major innovations. Hence, it is not surprising that the university which is a centre of knowledge and technology generation becomes increasingly essential for innovation and economic growth, too. Last, it is also common sense that knowledge generation and the innovation process itself is not a result of isolated agents either. Thus, collaborating for knowledge has also received broad support in the literature. Archibugi and Coco (2004) have, for example, pointed to the fact that collaborations might help to handle the ever more complex and therefore costly scientific problems.

In order to proof or disprove above findings regarding the publication, patenting and collaboration behaviour of the German universities, the following hypothesis is derived as follows:

Hypothesis 1: *Scientific publications and patent applications have highly increased over time and collaborations for knowledge and innovation have become much more important.*

Hypothesis 1 provides a first overview of the overall publication and patenting activity of the German universities and points subsequently to the highly growing collaborations of the German universities. Thereby, the knowledge linkages are illustrated by the increased number of co-authored publications, especially in contrast to single-authored publications. It is further illustrated how the German universities have developed from merely inventors to applicants themselves, pictured through the increasing number of patent applications. In this context, the rising collaboration potential concerning patents is pictured through the increasing number of co-applicants.

Besides, not only the heterogeneity in the landscape of knowledge generation has highly increased over the past years, but also the universities' former role as knowledge producer has shifted towards a role as knowledge mediator. Thus, universities have highly intensified their collaborations with other universities, public research institutes and enterprises' R&D divisions (Godin and Gingras 2000). In this context, among all possible collaborations, university-university linkages are still and by far the most important ones, but university-industry interactions have developed in a more dynamic way (Stephan 1996, Mansfield and Lee 1996 and Schartinger et al. 2002). Jaffe (1989) has, for example, already discovered by the end of the 1980s that a greater number of patents are generated when business is located in close proximity. Becker (2003) has stated that several studies have found out that joint research with universities increases the probability of firms to be engaged in the development of new products and technologies. Mansfield and Lee (1996) have further illustrated that universities cited by firms tend to be the leading generators of new fundamental knowledge. Finally, with respect to the co-authored publications, a vast majority of nowadays literature confirms that the use of academic knowledge is decisive for innovation and growth by means of new theoretical insights and expertise of a kind that enterprises find difficult to provide themselves with (Mansfield 1998, Cohen, Nelson and Walsh 2002).

With respect to these concerns, the following hypothesis is developed as follows:

Hypothesis 2: *The role of the German universities has changed from merely knowledge producers towards knowledge mediators, which leads to an increasing importance of universities as a central node for knowledge and innovation transfer.*

First of all, an illustration of the institutional distribution of the German university co-authors is presented. Thus, it is shown how the German universities' linkages to other institutional partners (themselves included) have developed over the past ten years, and to what extent they have highly increased not only the important linkages to 'knowledge institutions'[45], but also to industry partners. In terms of patent applications, it is rather shown how the co-applicants of the German universities have developed over time, pointing to the ever more increasing importance of industry partners in this regard. As each co-author as well as each co-applicant possesses its particular actor's code, it is possible to demonstrate the development of the institutional distribution of all German university cooperation partners.

Further, it is shown whether third-party funds have had a significant effect on the cooperation activity of the German universities with

[45] In this context, knowledge institution refers not only to universities but also to research institutes as both are highly engaged in knowledge-intensive tasks.

enterprises.[46] In order to evaluate this concern, an ordinary least squares (OLS) regression model is applied. Thus, it is proved whether third party funds *(thirdPF)*, administrative income *(admIncome)*, investment expenditure *(Invest)* and the number of professors *(Prof)* are responsible for the increasing rate of their cooperation activity. The model makes use of panel data of four years, and five time periods respectively[47], for all 76 German universities and is constituted as follows:

$$Pub_i/Pat_i = \beta_0 + \beta_1 thirdPF_i + \beta_2 admIncome_i + \beta_3 Invest_i + \beta_4 Prof + \delta EliteUni + \delta TUUni + \delta MedUni + \delta SizeUni + \varepsilon_i$$

where δ is the coefficient of the dummy variable and ε_i the disruptive factor. As can be seen from the formula, four dummy variables are integrated in order to proof whether significance lies in the dummy variable itself or not.

Afterwards, by means of SNA, it is illustrated how the German universities are already linked in the chains of contact, i.e. how many distinct cooperation partners exist and how the importance of a university as a mediator has developed over the past ten years. For doing this, the values of normalized degree and betweenness centrality

[46] In the case of patent applications, it is proved whether third-party funds have had a significant effect on their overall patenting activity.

[47] For the publications, the years 2000, 2003, 2006 and 2009 has been taken; in the case of the patents, four time periods have been developed, namely 1999-2000, 2001-2002, 2003-2004, 2005-2006 and 2007-2008.

are chosen as they well indicate how central each university lies in the knowledge and innovation networks pictured through co-authorships and co-applicants.

7.2. Proximity Patterns in Times of Globalisation

The question to what extent these collaborations benefit from the proximity of partners has been a major subject of the scientific debate in the field of economic geography and knowledge and innovation economics for decades. Empirical evidence on this issue is manifold. A vast majority of that literature still suggests that the diffusion of knowledge highly clusters geographically, i.e. they have pointed to the fact that knowledge spillovers are rather found within a short distance. Audretsch (1998), for example, has highlighted that the diffusion of knowledge from the university that creates that knowledge to any other institutional partners tends to be spatially restricted. Besides, there are several studies that have further identified localized knowledge spillovers based on patent data, innovation counts or co-authored publications (Jaffe et al. 1993, Anselin et al. 1997 and McKelvey et al. 2003). Last, Zucker et al. (2001) have shown that biotechnology firms are strongly influenced by the location of successful giants in academic research institutions. In contrast, another strand of literature questions the importance of geographical distance and refers to the development of modern ICT that facilitates cooperation among distant partners and enables them to efficiently interact without face to face contacts. In this context, it is video-conferencing or the possibility to share ideas via computer-mediated technology that makes the knowledge generating process less dependent from spatial proximity (Hancock and Dunham 2001 and Wainfan and Davis 2004). Further, empirical findings have shown in the case of university-industry interaction that global cooperation is more common than regional collaborations (Audretsch and Stephan 1996, McKelvey et al. 2003). Arundel and Geuna (2004) have further illustrated that firms interested in codified knowledge, e.g. in terms of patents or publications, are less likely to perceive geographic distance a barrier. The same applied to university-university linkages as Archibugi and Coco (2004) have found a dramatic increase in the internationally co-authored publications which has been also facilitated by the strong diffusion of information and communication technologies.

Being aware of above findings, the following hypothesis is set up:

Hypothesis 3: *Spatial Proximity has lost in importance regarding close network collaborations concerning knowledge spillovers between the German universities and other institutional cooperation partners.*

First of all, it is shown to what extent proximity still matters by considering all German university co-authors that are within the 1,000 km corridor as described above. In this context, it is also illustrated how the institutional cooperation partners of the German universities are spatially distributed. For doing this, Spearman's rank correlation coefficient is used to shed light on the distance pattern. Spearman's rank correlation coefficient is a non-parametric measure of correlation, using ranks to calculate the correlation and looks as follows:

$$r_s = \frac{\sum_i (x_i - \bar{x})\,(y_i - \bar{y})}{\sqrt{\sum_i (x_i - \bar{x})^2 \sum_i (y_i - \bar{y})^2}}$$

It shows the direction of association between any two variables x and y. If x tends to increase when y increases, the coefficient of Spearman's rank correlation is positive. The other way round, if x is likely to decrease when y increases, the Spearman correlation coefficient is negative (Bosch 1996). Second, by means of the cluster analysis, it is illustrated how all German university co-authors are spatially distributed, either being regionally located or supra-regionally located. Last, an overview of the spatial distribution depending on where the co-authors are coming from is demonstrated in order to show how they are worldwide presented.

To sum up, chapter seven provides a detailed overview and impression of the development path of the publication and patenting activity of all German universities as well as of their cooperation potential, especially with regard to the institutional distribution of their cooperation partners. This chapter is rounded up with first reflections regarding the spatial distribution of the German university co-authors in general, bringing up first statements regarding nowadays importance of spatial proximity.

8. Empirical Results regarding the Knowledge Generation, Innovation and Collaboration Potential of the German Universities

Chapter eight starts with the empirical results of this PhD thesis, beginning with the comprehensive analysis regarding the publication, patenting and collaboration behaviour of the German universities. Further, it points to proximity patterns in times of globalisation and explores how the German universities behave in this regard.

8.1. Knowledge Generation and Collaboration

The first analysis explores in how far the publication activity of the German universities has increased over the past ten years. Thus, the following figure simply illustrates this development in absolute numbers and simultaneously points to the extensive self-developed data set in this regard:

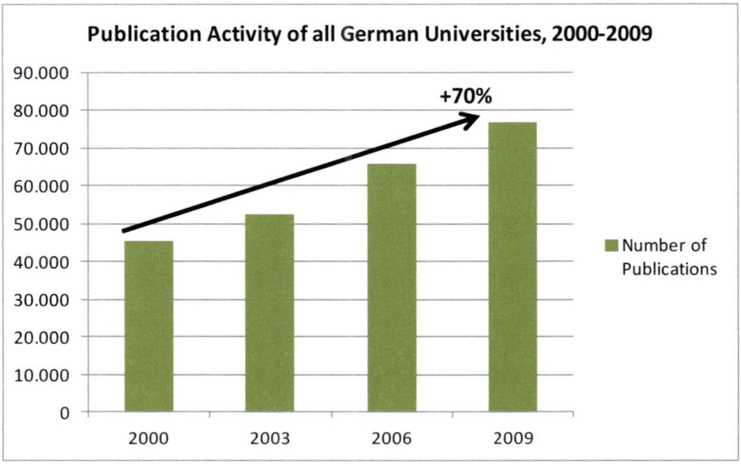

Figure 11: Publication Activity of all German Universities, absolute Numbers, 2000-2009 (own illustration).

At the first glance, it is obvious that all analyses regarding knowledge generation and collaboration can make use of around 250,000 single publications where at least one German university is involved with for a time period from 2000 until 2009. Thus, there is no doubt that the German universities are highly involved in scientific papers, here with regard to the Scopus data-base. While they have been involved in around 44,000 publications within the first time period, they could already record about 80,000 publications in 2009. Thereby, the highest increase has occurred from the second to the third time period, making up 30% of the overall change. Generally, the German universities could increase their number of publications from the first to the last time period by around 70%.

Being aware of the enormous increase of the German universities output in scientific papers, the next step consists of the presentation of the development path of their collaboration activity. Hence, the following figure indicates to what extent the German universities are already involved in close network collaborations which are pictured through co-authorships:

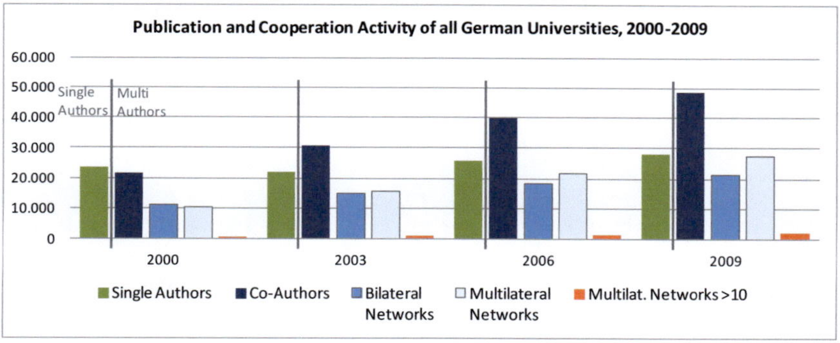

Figure 12: Publication and Cooperation Activity of all German Universities, absolute Numbers, 2000-2009 (own illustration).

The figure demonstrates that within the first time period, about 23,000 publications have been published by the German universities where only one single person has been involved with. In contrast, at the same time, the German universities have published about 21,000 publications which have been co-authored. Thus, in 2000, the German universities have still published more often on their own than to go into a cooperation. Overall, as Figure 12 already indicates, on average, around 44,000 publications have been published during the first time period.

But, while single-authorship has even declined from the first to the second time period, co-authorship has risen about 42% during that time. Further, in 2009, the German universities were overall engaged in almost 80,000 publications at all, but only about 28,000 have come from single-authorship. Thus, publication and collaboration activity continuously rose over the time period from 2000 until 2009, whereas it is very striking that single-authorship has become much less important over the past ten years. From the first to the fourth time period, single-authorship has increased by only 18%, while co-authorship has risen by 125%.

With regard to the structure of the co-authored publications, it is also obvious that the number of bilateral and multilateral networks is almost equal within the first time period. In 2000, there are around 11,000 bilateral networks and about 10,500 networks where more than two authors have participated. But, while the share of bilateral networks has not even doubled from the first to the fourth time period, networks with more than two authors have risen by almost 170% during that time period. Last, networks with more than 10 authors can be rather neglected in this regard, even though they have increased by 250%; their overall share has just made up three per cent of all networks considered within the last time period. However, it can be concluded that not only co-authorship has become much more important during the past ten years, but also all those networks with more than two but less than ten participating authors.

In order to underpin the finding that single-authorship has become much less important over the past ten years compared to co-authorship, a box plot is illustrated in the following, which visualizes again above findings:

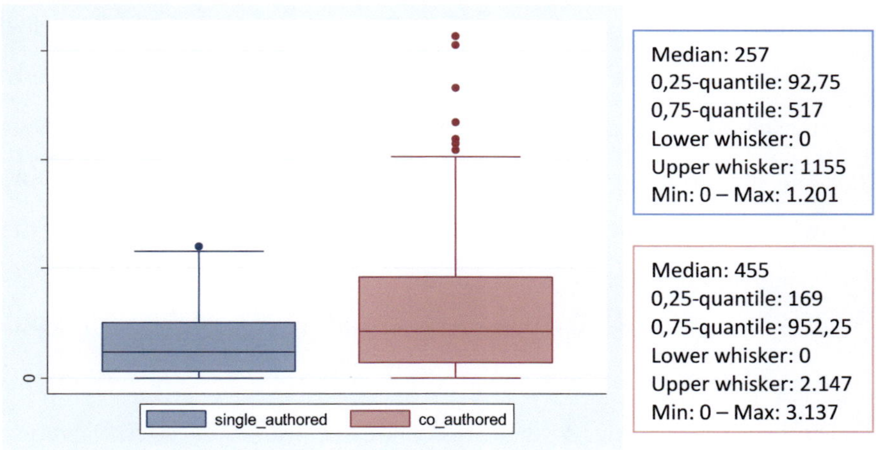

Figure 13: Box plot of the Publication Activity of all German Universities, single-authorship vs. co-authorship, 1999-2010 (created by means of STATA).

While on the left side, the distribution of single-authored publications is illustrated, the right side presents the distribution of the co-authored publications. Generally, the box plot delivers a variety of robust measures of variation and location; thus, the table on the right hand side illustrates the median, the upper and lower quartiles, the upper and lower whiskers which define what is commonly referred to as the upper inner and lower inner fence values and the outliers of both distributions for a time period from 2000 until 2009.

Comparing both measures, it is again very obvious that the German universities are much more engaged in cooperation activities in the meantime, as the median of the co-authored distribution is 455 compared to 257 of the single-authored ones. But not only has the median indicated this finding, but also the 0.25- and 0.75-quantiles. While within the group of single-authored publications 25% lie below 92.75 and 25% above 517, both values are much higher in the case of the co-authored publications, namely 25% below 169 and 25% above 952.25. The lower whisker is zero for both distributions, but the upper whisker is for the co-authored publications twice as high as for the single-authored ones. As there are outliners in both data sets, the distance between the highest value of single-authored and co-authored publications is even larger; the highest value of co-authored publications is three times as big as the highest value of single-authored publications. Thus, it is again highly obvious that close network collaborations have much more increased as could be especially seen by the illustration of above box plot.

Up to this point, it is well established that the publication and cooperation activity of the German universities has highly increased over the past ten years. Overall, they could increase their number of publications from the first to the last time period by around 70%. Further, the collaboration activity of the German universities continuously rose over the time period from 2000 until 2009, as single-authorship has only increased by 18%, while co-authorship has risen by 125%. Thus, hypothesis 1a is confirmed by above findings.

A second step now explores in how far the role of the German universities has changed from solely knowledge producers towards knowledge mediators, which, in turn, leads to an increasing importance of the German universities as a central node for knowledge transfer. Before coming to this concern, an illustration of the institutional distribution of the German university co-authors is firstly presented by the following figure:

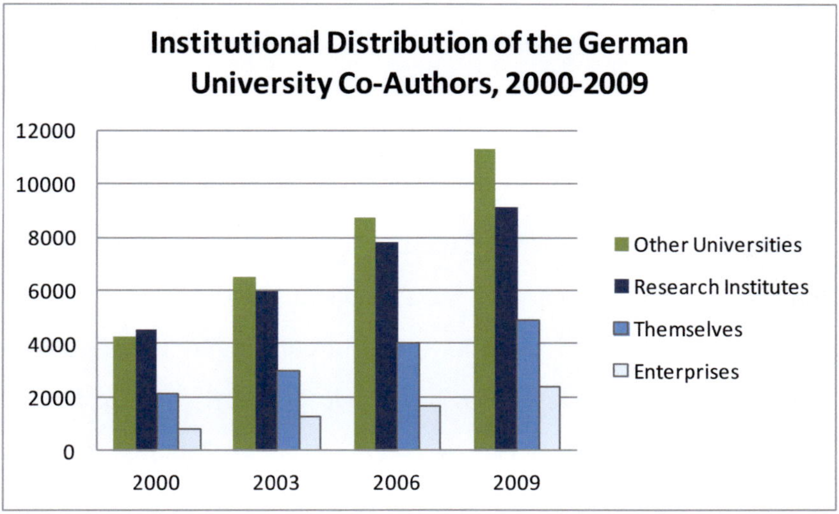

Figure 14: Institutional Distribution of the German University Co-Authors, weighted Numbers, 2000-2009 (own illustration).

As can be seen from the figure, the German universities are either linked to other universities[48], to research institutes, to themselves or to enterprises. First of all, it is obvious that all four network constellations have highly increased over the past ten years, even though one group has grown stronger than one another. The strongest network can be found between the German universities and other universities. Even though these collaborations have occupied only second place within the first time period with around 4,300 linkages, they have risen by 166% to around 11,400 linkages. The group of research institutes is also very strong; they have had 4,500 linkages to the German universities within the first time period, and could increase their network collaborations by 102% up to 9,200 linkages within the last time period. However, compared to the group of other universities, they have lost some places in this regard. Thus, knowledge networks with other universities could highly catch up with the research institutes, being nowadays even much stronger than the research institutes. It is also obvious that the German universities have cooperated quite frequently with themselves, too. Within the first period, there have been around 2,100 linkages among the German universities which have risen by 130% to around 4,900 linkages. However, the weakest group of network collaborations seems to be the group of the enterprises, as they have started quite low with only around 800 linkages. But, it is very eye-catching that they could increase their linkages to the German universities by incredible 212% up

[48] In this context, universities include all domestic and foreign universities except of the 76 German universities that are subject of study.

to 2,400 linkages. Thus, these network collaborations possess the highest rate of increase among all groups.

In this context, it can be carefully concluded that network collaborations with universities are most important, but, university-industry linkages have had a more dynamic development as they could have been increased by incredible 212% up to 2,400 which has made up the highest increase among all collaboration partners. One reason for this could be that enterprises have sometimes problems to provide themselves with the scientific knowledge they need, and thus, looking for university partners themselves, too.

Further, being aware of the overall dynamic development of the German university collaborations to other institutional partners in general, it is further interesting to explore how the role of the German universities as knowledge mediators has developed over time. In order to evaluate the increasing importance of the German universities as central nodes for knowledge transfer, the values of normalized degree and betweenness centrality are used. By means of normalized degree centrality, it is shown how the German universities have developed over the past ten years regarding their distinct cooperation partners[49]. Further, betweenness centrality illustrates how the German universities

[49] In this context, distinct cooperation partners mean that double counts do not occur, i.e. if a German university is linked to the same enterprise several times, this cooperation is only counted once.

are already linked in the chains of contacts as it measures how often a German university lies on the shortest way between two other actors.

First of all, the following table shows the mean values of normalized degree centrality of all German universities:

Mean Value of normalized Degree Centrality of the German Universities, 2000-2009			
2000	2003	2006	2009
0,01916411	0,01951526	0,02095905	0,02246344

Table 10: Mean Value of normalized Degree Centrality of the German Universities, 2000-2009 (own illustration).

The table shows that the German universities have highly increased their distinct cooperation partners over the past ten years, as the value has risen by around 20%. Thereby, the top three German universities in 2009 are Heidelberg (0.091701), the Technical University of Munich (0.0865566) and the LMU Munich (0.796075), while the University of Koblenz-Landau, the University of Weimar and the University of Bamberg are the top three regarding the highest increase over the past ten years. However, the following table now points to the mean value of betweenness centrality of the German universities from 2000 until 2009, thus illustrating how all German universities have developed on average in this regard:

Mean Value of Betweenness Centrality of the German Universities, 2000-2009			
2000	2003	2006	2009
0,02640125	0,02527691	0,02464999	0,0243337

Table 11: Mean Value of Betweenness Centrality of the German Universities, 2000-2009 (own illustration).

At the first glance, it is eye-catching that the value of betweenness centrality has not increased over the past ten years, but decreased from around 0.026 to 0.024[50]. As the value of normalized degree centrality[51] has generally developed the other way round, one may assume that while some of the German universities have gained in importance as knowledge mediators, others might have lost some places in this regard. Another reason can be given by the fact that more German universities have gained in importance regarding their number of distinct cooperation partners, thus, the network has become larger but not automatically tighter so that some of the German universities have received smaller values regarding their importance as mediator. Anyway, the top three universities in 2009 in this regard consist again of the University of Heidelberg (0.097603), the Technical University of Munich (0.086908) and the LMU Munich (0.078098), while the University of Koblenz-Landau, the University of Bamberg and the University of Weimar are the top three regarding the highest increase

[50] 43 of the German universities have had decreasing values in this regard.
[51] 28 of the German universities have had decreasing values in this regard.

over the past ten years. A detailed examination of the distinct groups of German universities, pointing to significant differences in their behavioural patterns can be found in chapter ten.

Hence, as the German universities have indeed highly increased their distinct cooperation partners over the past ten years at the expense of possible loops within the networks, hypothesis 2a is only largely confirmed.

Finally, bearing in mind that university-industry linkages have experienced the most dynamic development, the OLS regression model explores whether the increasing cooperation activity of the German universities with enterprises has been affected by third-party funds or not. The following table now illustrates the results of the model[52]:

[52] Test of multi-collinearity has been made; all mentioned variables do not have a strong correlation to each other. Further, the residuals are normally distributed and possess homogeneity of variance.

VARIABLES	Number of Enterprise Interactions
Investment Expenditure	1.67e-08
	(2.96e-08)
Administrative Income	2.32e-07***
	(4.47e-08)
Third-Party Funds	2.22e-07***
	(2.44e-08)
Professors	-0.00421
	(0.00522)
Dummy [Elite]	-0.511
	(2.268)
Dummy [TU]	2.417
	(2.169)
Dummy [Med]	2.489
	(1.751)
Dummy [Size]	4.146*
	(2.383)
Constant	-0.350
	(1.685)
Observations	304
R-squared	0.696

Standard errors in parentheses
*** p<0.01, ** p<0.05, * p<0.1

Table 12: Results of the OLS-Regression Model – Number of Enterprise Interactions (own illustration).

The table now expresses to what extent the above independent variables affect the publication activity of the German universities, especially with regard to third party funds. It shows that third-party funds and administrative income highly affect their collaboration activities with enterprises. For both variables, the result is highly significant with a standard error less than 1%. Referring to both coefficients, it is obvious that their values are particularly small. However, this finding is not too extraordinary as the size of third-party funds and administrative income is extremely high compared to the number of publications. Hence, in case of an increase of third-party funds or administrative income in the amount of one unit, the number of publications would, of course, only increase very slightly as the coefficients indicate. Reasons for the significance of third party funds can be constituted in the fact that most of those funds have come from the private economy which, in turn, has led to more collaborations and co-authored publications. Besides, the variable administrative income includes all supplied services as any income from hospital treatment, from sales of goods of any agricultural test materials or from the sale of any tangible assets. Thus, it is possible that the German universities have closely worked with enterprises concerning above supplied services which, in turn, has also led to more co-authored publications, too. Besides, it is interesting to notice that there is also a significant result for one dummy variable, namely the size-dummy with a standard error less than 10%. From this it can be concluded that the number of co-authored publications with enterprises increases with the size of the university.

8.2. Innovation and Collaboration

The second line of thought builds upon the changing role of the German universities as more entrepreneurial institutions, using patent applications to illustrate their changing role within innovation patterns.

First of all, it should be mentioned that the scope of the data set is many times smaller than the one of the publications. In total, the amount of the patent data makes up only 1% of the one of the publications[53], as the following figure indicates:

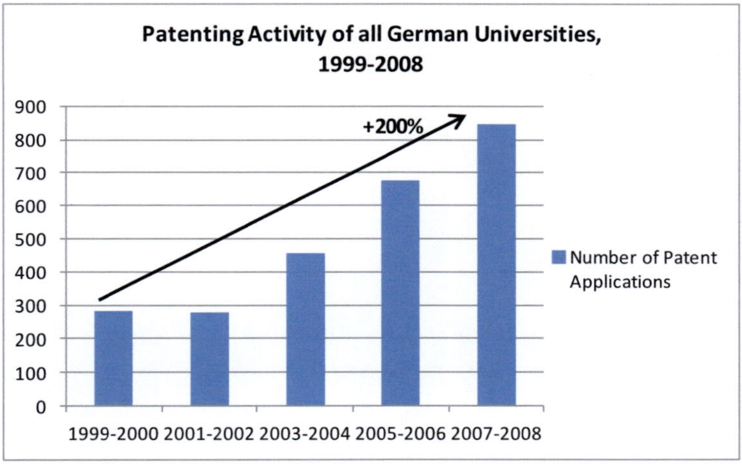

Figure 15: Patenting Activity of all German Universities, absolute Numbers, 1999-2008 (own illustration).

Figure 15 illustrates the overall patenting activity of the German universities from 1999 until 2008 as it has been done for the scientific publications. It shows that after a small decline of patent applications

[53] The classical German university is actually known as a knowledge-intensive institution that is highly engaged in scientific papers, but less in innovation output pictured through patent applications. Therefore, the differences in the scope of data are still prevalent and not uncommon.

from the first to the second time period[54], the German universities have experienced a huge increase regarding their number of filed patents. While they have filed around 281 patents from 1999 until 2000, they could already triple their number of patent applications within the last time period.

As a patent does not only include applicants but inventors too (see chapter four), it is further interesting to illustrate how many patents exist in total where any German university has been involved with, either being applicant or inventor[55]:

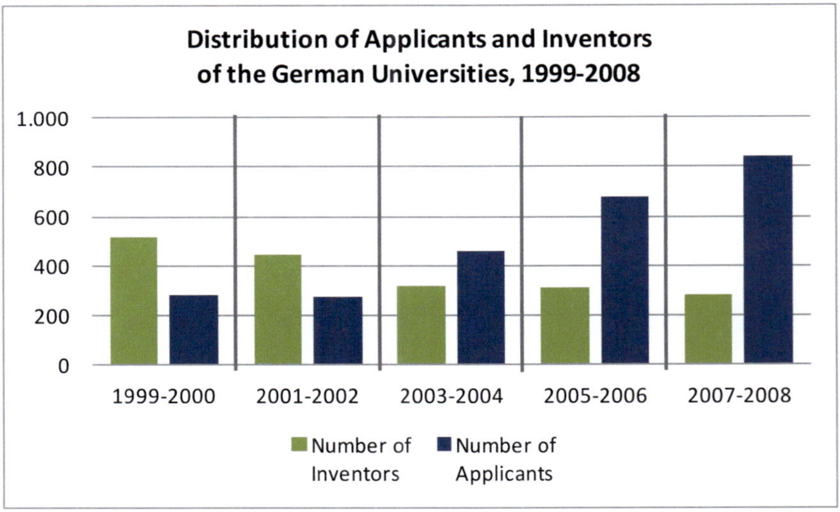

[54] The decline from the first to the second period has probably been occurred due to the dot.com bubble which was a historic speculative bubble covering the end of the nineties (1997 – 2000). The burst of the bubble took place during 2000-2001.

[55] In a few cases, the German university is applicant and inventor at the same time. Figure 16 anyway indicates that the patenting behaviour of the German universities has changed from merely inventors to more likely applicants.

Figure 16: Distribution of Applicants and Inventors of the German Universities, absolute Numbers, 1999-2008 (own illustration).

It can be well observed that while the number of applicants has generally increased over the past ten years, the number of inventors has developed the opposite way. It is striking that the German universities have started quite strong to operate as inventor on a patent. From 1999 until 2000, over 500 inventors could be recorded, while within the last time period, there have only been about 280 patents where at least one German university has been registered as inventor, which makes up a decrease of over 50%. Of course, as the overall patenting activity of all German universities has increased over the past ten years, the development path of the number of applicants looks the other way round as Figure 16 indicates. Thus, one can already conclude that the behaviour of the German universities has strongly changed over the past ten years, as they operate much more often as applicants themselves, hence, being less dependent on other institutional actors anymore.

Reasons for this opposite development lie possibly in the fact that the so called German 'Hochschullehrerprivileg' prevailed until February 2002. This means that after 2002 employees of universities (professors or scientific assistants) could not anymore dispose freely of their intellectual property rights. Thus, before 2002, it is possible that in case the professor or any scientific assistant cooperated with any other institution possessed a kind of weaker position as private person when it went along the question who should operate as applicant and who as inventor on the patent.[56] On the other side, from February 2002 onwards, the university itself appears frequently as applicant itself when a professor or scientific assistant invent anything which is worth for a patent.[57]

Coming now to the development path of the cooperation activity of all German universities, it can be stated that it is generally unusual to operate as exclusive applicant on a patent, as at least one or two further inventors are regularly also involved within a patent application. For example, from 1999 until 2008, there are only about 100 patents where only one German university is recorded as exclusive applicant, with no other inventors on it except of itself. However, this PhD thesis concentrates on co-applicant networks in order to show the development path of their cooperation activities in this regard. The following figure firstly shows the increasing number of co-applicants of the German universities from 1999 until 2008:

[56] Exclusive applicants can freely dispose of their patent and of course of its possible revenues, too.

[57] All further analyses with regard to cooperation patterns will refer to co-applicant networks.

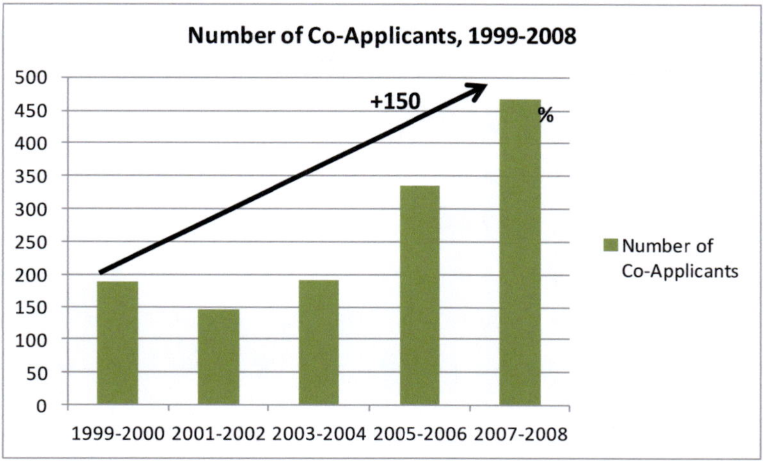

Figure 17: Number of Co-Applicants, absolute Numbers, 1999-2008 (own illustration).

As can be seen from the figure, the number of the German university co-applicants has highly increased over the past ten years, except of a small decline from the first to the second time period. However, this decrease is not surprising as the number of filed patents has also declined from 1999/2000 until 2001/2002. Overall, the German universities have seen an increase of around 150% during the past ten years, while the largest rise has occurred from the third to the fourth time period by around 80%. Overall, it can be stated that not only the patenting activity of the German universities in terms of filed patents has highly increased over the past ten years, but the number of co-applicants, too.

Up to this point, it is well shown that not only the number of filed patents has highly increased over past ten years, but also the cooperation activity of the German universities as illustrated by the rising number of co-applicants. Overall, they could even triple their number of patent applications, thus operating much more often as applicants themselves so that they are less dependent on other institutional actors anymore. Hence, hypothesis 1 is also confirmed in terms of patents by above findings.

Finally, it is also shown how the co-applicants of the German universities are institutional distributed over the past ten years as the following figure illustrates:

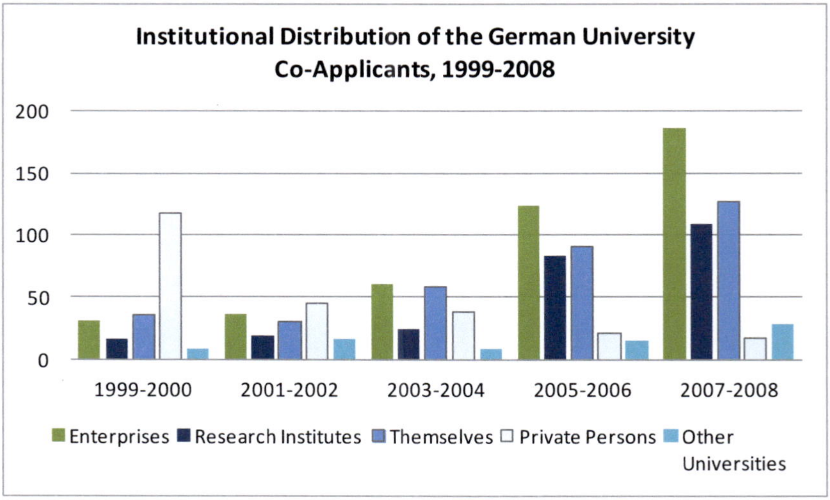

Figure 18: Institutional Distribution of the German University Co-Applicants, absolute Numbers, 1999-2008 (own illustration).

First of all, the aforementioned opposite development can be confirmed through the above figure as a highly increasing trend of almost all possible co-applicants can be observed. Only the development path of the private persons looks differently. While they have made up the highest share of co-applicants from 1999 until 2000, they have strongly decreased over the past ten years (minus 85%). In this context, one can assume that almost all private persons have been working at the same German university as the co-applicant, too. Thus, while the German universities have been working more or less 'alone' on a patent within the first time period, they have really changed their cooperation manner during the past ten years, as they have increasingly worked with other institutional partners.

Coming to the institutional distribution of the German university co-applicants, it is obvious that they have most often cooperated with enterprises. Within the first time period, they have had 31 enterprises as co-applicants, and from 2007 until 2008, they have already cooperated with 187 enterprises (plus 500%). The highest increase of co-applicants from the first to the last time period can be observed within the group of research institutes (plus 540%), even though the absolute number of those partnerships is always much lower compared to the one of the enterprises. Besides, the group of German universities as co-applicants is also very strong. Within the first time period, they have even made up the highest share of co-applicants, but have developed slower than the enterprises. Thus, within the last time period, they have occupied second place between the enterprises and the research institutes. Overall, the German universities could raise the share of cooperating with themselves by 250%. Last, the share of other universities as co-applicants has also increased by 250%, but anyway, it has just made up 6% of all possible co-applicants within the last time period.

Further, being aware of the dynamic development of the German university interactions especially to enterprises, research institutes and to themselves, it is further interesting to examine how the role of the German universities as innovative mediators has developed over time. Thus, as it has been done for the scientific publications, the values of normalized degree and betweenness centrality are used to evaluate the increasing importance of the German universities as central nodes for innovation transfer[58]. First of all, the following table shows the mean values of the normalized degree centrality of all German universities:

Mean Value of normalized Degree Centrality of the German Universities, 1999-2008		
1999/2000	2003/2004	2007/2008
0,006309635	0,006600662	0,013698011

Table 13: Mean Value of normalized Degree Centrality of the German Universities, 1999-2008 (own illustration).

[58] It has to be mentioned in this regard that some of the German universities are not at all involved in innovation networks, while others still possess null values regarding the value of betweenness centrality.

As in the case of publication data, above table also well documents for the patents that the German universities have highly increased their distinct co-applicants over the past ten years, as the value has enlarged by around 120%. Thus, the dynamics regarding the development of the number of distinct co-applicants is much higher compared to the one of the co-authors. Of course, in terms of absolute numbers, both distributions cannot be compared with each other at all. However, the top three German universities within the last time period are Erlangen-Nürnberg (0.0608496), Würzburg (0.0608696) and the Karlsruhe Institute of Technology (KIT) (0.0521739), while the University of Freiburg, the University of Hamburg and the University of Erlangen-Nürnberg are the top three regarding the highest increase over the past ten years.

At the first glance, it is obvious that the German universities possess different behavioural patterns regarding their publication and patenting activities. This important finding will be discussed later on within the final conclusion and reflection.

Further, the following table points to the mean values of betweenness centrality of the German universities from 1999 until 2008, thus illustrating how all German universities have developed on average in this regard:

Mean Value of Betweenness Centrality of the German Universities, 1999-2008		
1999/2000	2003/2004	2007/2008
0,000135372	0,00013266	0,014757969

Table 14: Mean Value of Betweenness Centrality of the German Universities, 1999-2008 (own illustration).

It can be seen that the value of betweenness centrality has increased over the past ten years, differently from the mean value of the betweenness centrality in terms publications. Anyway, the top three universities within the last time period in this regard consist of the KIT (0.115064), Erlangen-Nürnberg (0.0896877) and the Technical University of Munich (0.0652174), while the LMU Munich, the University of Würzburg and the Technical University of Aachen are the top three regarding the highest increase over the past ten years. A detailed examination of the distinct groups of German universities, pointing to significant differences in their behavioural patterns can be found in chapter ten.

To exemplarily show how a co-applicant network looks like, the following figure illustrates the network of the best-performing university regarding the value of betweenness centrality; thus, it is the co-applicant network of the KIT:

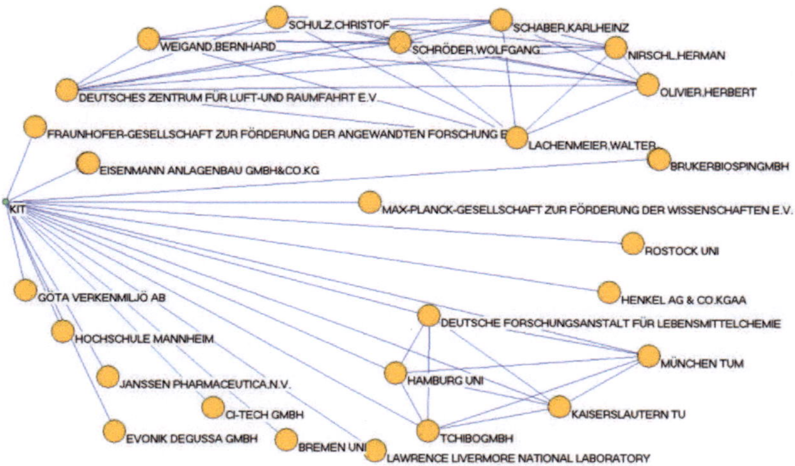

Figure 19: Co-Applicant Network of the KIT, 2007-2008 (own illustration).

Overall, a strongly growing importance of the German universities as co-applicants in innovation networks can be generally observed over the past ten years, especially with regard to close network collaborations with enterprises. Hence, hypothesis 2b is also confirmed in terms of patents.

Finally, bearing in mind that industry as well as research linkages has gained in importance over the past ten years, it is again reasonable to ask whether third-party funds have had a significant effect on the collaboration activity of the German universities in general. Hence, above mentioned OLS regression model is applied. The following table now illustrates the results of the model[59]:

VARIABLES	Patenting Activity
Investment Expenditure	1.78e-09
	(2.12e-08)
Administrative Income	2.61e-08
	(3.15e-08)
Third-Party Funds	7.39e-08***
	(1.84e-08)
Professors	-0.00177
	(0.00206)
Dummy [Elite]	7.592***
	(1.602)
Dummy [TU]	0.703
	(1.538)
Dummy [Med]	-1.354
	(1.246)
Dummy [Size]	2.814*
	(1.637)
Constant	0.848
	(1.099)
Observations	304
R-squared	0.411

Standard errors in parentheses
*** p<0.01, ** p<0.05, * p<0.1

Table 15: Results of the OLS-Regression Model – Development of the Patenting Activity (own illustration).

The table demonstrates to what extent the four independent variables affect the cooperation activity of the German universities regarding joint patent applications. Thereby, it shows that third-party funds have highly affected the patenting behaviour of the German universities over the

[59] Test of multi-collinearity has been made; all mentioned variables do not have a strong correlation to each other. Further, the residuals are normally distributed and possess homogeneity of variance.

past ten years; the result is significant with a standard error less than 1%. Referring to its coefficient, it is again obvious that the value is extremely small. However, as it has been already discussed within the part of the publication analysis in this regard, this result is not too extraordinary as the size of third-party funds is extremely high compared to the number of patent applications. Hence, in case of an increase of third-party funds in the amount of one unit, the number of patent application would hardly change. Nevertheless, the reasons for the significance of the variable can be explained in the fact that the German universities have strongly cooperated with enterprises which are, for example, external funding sources. Further, it is interesting to notice that there are significant results for two of the four dummy variables, too, namely for the elite-universities as well as for the size dummy. For the elite-universities, the significance is on a 99% level. From this, it can be drawn that all significant results are rooted in this special type of university. Last, the size dummy also possesses a slight significant result with a standard error less than 10%. Thus, the size of a German university positively affects the number of co-applicants itself, too.

Hypothesis 2b is also confirmed in terms of patents as third-party funds have had a positive significant effect on the patenting activity of the German universities.

8.3. Proximity Patterns in Times of Globalization

This subchapter deals with the comprehensive analysis of the spatial examination with regard to the publication behaviour of the German universities as already illustrated within the part on the methodology. As already brought up, in times of globalisation it is of high interest to explore whether proximity still matters as much as it did years before. Thus, the following figure gives a first overview of the spatial distribution of the co-authors of all German universities within the 1,000 km radius for 2000 and 2009:

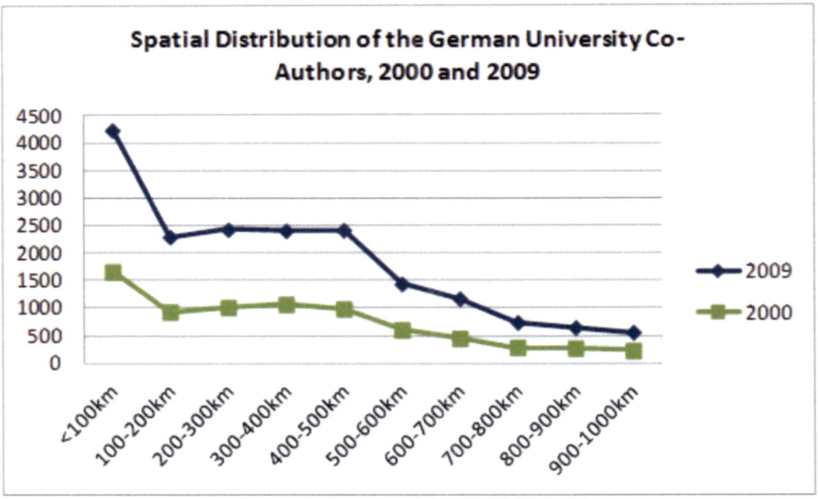

Figure 20: Spatial Distribution of the German University Co-Authors (100 km Corridor) weighted Numbers, 2000 and 2009 (own illustration).

First of all, this kind of illustration also emphasises the fact that the German university co-authors within the 1.000 km radius have highly increased over the past ten years. *Second*, at the first glance, it also seems very obvious that local co-authors who are within a radius of 100 km are especially important for the German universities as potential cooperation partners. This finding might be also confirmed by the huge increase of these partners from 2000 until 2009. While in 2000 about 1,655 partners have been located very close to the German universities, in 2009 already 4,233 co-authors have been located within the radius of 100 km which makes up an increase of 155%. The other distance corridors have not been able to show such strong increase rates. *Third*, while the co-authors did not decline that much from the first to the second distance corridor in 2000, in 2009 only half as much co-authors are in the second corridor compared to the first one. Further, another huge decline can be observed from the fifth to the second corridor which accounts for both time periods. In 2000, there were 986 co-authors recorded within the fifth corridor compared to only 600 within the sixth one which makes up a decline of 40%. The same finding accounts for 2009, too. Thus, it is not surprising that the conducted cluster analysis has found the average cut-off point at around 468 km. However, in general, it seems that the number of co-authors declines depending on the distance. In order to acquire a more valid estimation in this regard, a second distance corridor has been evolved which now covers 25 km each. Thus, the following figure shows again the spatial distribution of the German university co-authors for 2000 and 2009.

Further, the values of Spearman's rank correlation coefficient are listed for both years which can be used to statistically confirm the finding that geographical proximity still matters when those co-authors are considered that are within the radius of 1,000 km:

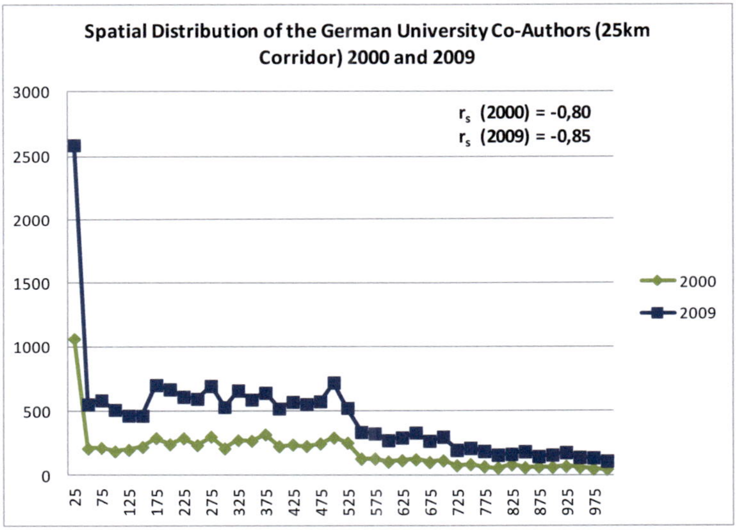

Figure 21: Spatial Distribution of the German University Co-Authors (25 km Corridor) weighted Numbers, 2000 and 2009 (own illustration).

Figure 21 emphasises even stronger that especially locality[60] still plays an important role for the German universities. It is very apparent that from 2000 until 2009 an increase of around 140% can be observed regarding all co-authors that are inside the 25 km corridor. Also the second stronger decline of co-authors can be still seen at the point of

---

[60] In this context, locality includes all co-authors that are within a radius of only 25 km.

around 500 km. Besides, the values of Spearman's rank correlation coefficient both show a quite strong and negative effect. In 2000, the value is -0.80 and in 2009 even -0.85. This means that the number of co-authors declines with the growth of distance.

However, according to figure 21, it can be assumed that locality highly matters while the German universities do not further consider distance for the choice of their co-authors when they are anywhere located between 25 km and approximately 475 km[61]. Afterwards, proximity seems to play a role again regarding the choice of cooperation partners as above figure indicates. Bearing this in mind, the following figure now firstly illustrates the spatial distribution of the German university co-authors between 25 km and <475 km:

[61] Figure 21 shows a second decline at approximately 475 km. Besides, the cluster analysis has also pointed to an average cut-off point of around 475 km (468 km).

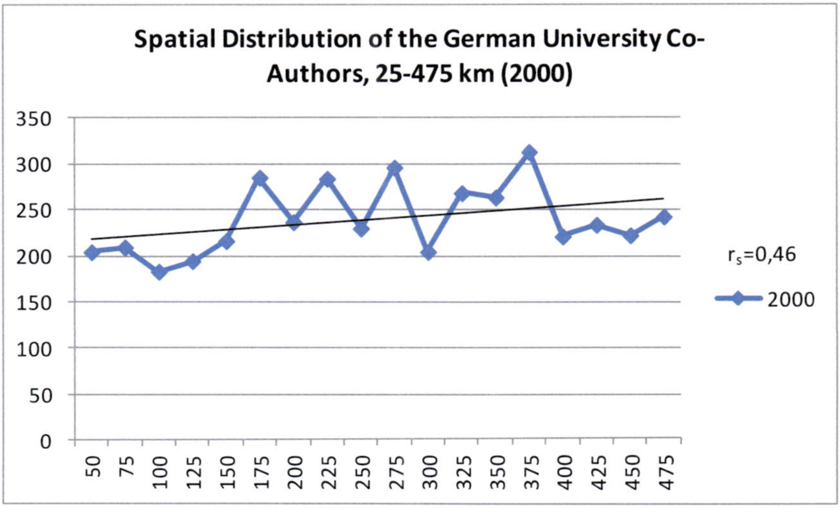

Figure 22: Spatial Distribution of the German University Co-Authors (25km - <475 km) weighted Numbers, 2000 (own illustration).

As can be seen from the figure, without the co-authors of the first distance corridor and without the co-authors that are farther away than 475 km, the German universities have not seen distance as a barrier, as spearman's rank correlation coefficient still shows a slight positive effect which means that the number of co-authors has even increased with the growth of distance (with p=0.05). Last, the following figure now illustrates the spatial distribution of the German university co-authors that are anywhere between 475 and 1,000 km located:

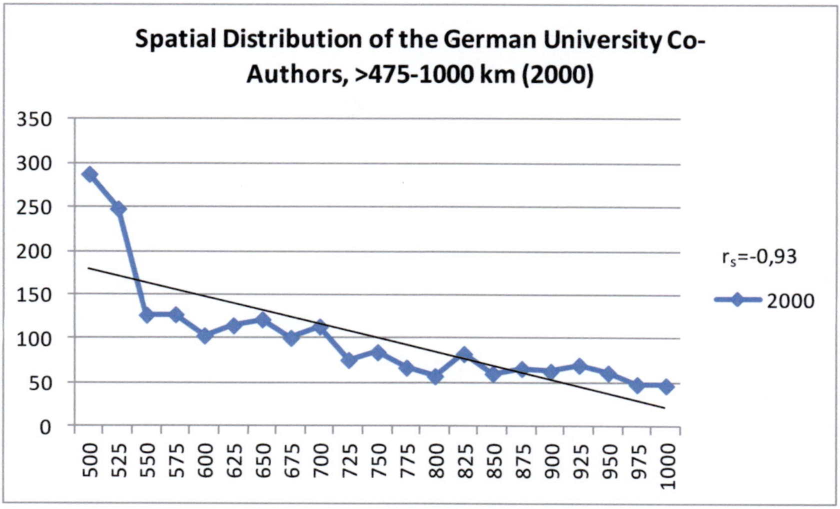

Figure 23: Spatial Distribution of the German University Co-Authors (475 km - 1.000 km) weighted Numbers, 2000 (own illustration).

Now, by means of above figure, it can be well seen that the number of cooperation partners has declined with the growth of distance as the value of Spearman's rank correlation coefficient is -0.93.

To sum up, while locality still seems to highly matter regarding the choice of the cooperation partners, regional distance of 25 km until <475 km does not seem to play a role, but from 475 km onwards the friction of distance have started weight again.

Further, it is aimed to present an overview of the spatial distribution of all German university co-authors, either being regional or supra-regional located (see again *chapter six* for the classification). Hence, not only the co-authors of the 1,000 km radius are considered, but also all others beyond. By means of the cluster analysis, the following figure shows the share of regional and supra-regional located cooperation partners for the time period from 2000 until 2009:

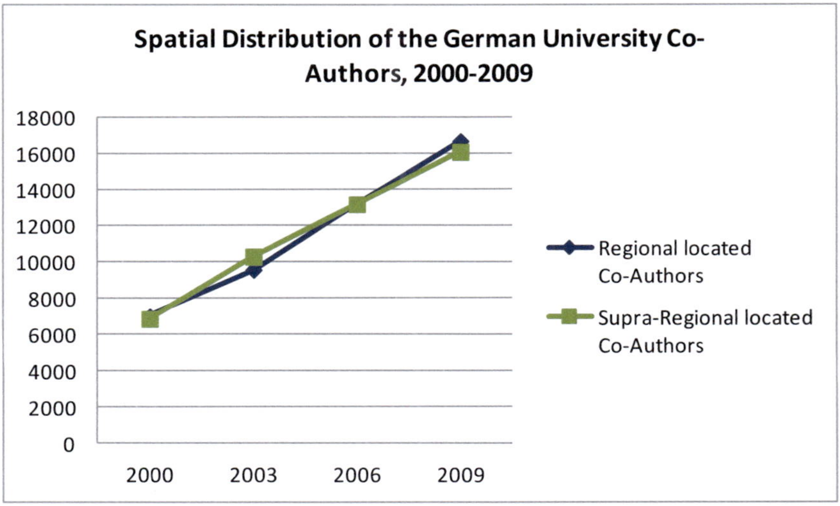

Figure 24: Spatial Distribution of the German University Co-Authors, weighted Numbers, 2000-2009 (own illustration).

As can be seen from the figure, the spatial distribution of the German university co-authors is more or less equally distributed when the classification of the cluster analysis is taken into account. Hence, around half of all co-authors are regionally located, i.e. they are located within a radius of around 468 km on average, and others that are farther in distance are considered to be supra-regionally[62] located partners. To sum up, considering all cooperation partners it has been shown that regionally and supra-regionally located partners are more or less equally important, even though today the number of the regionally located co-authors has slightly passed the supra-regionally located ones.

Finally, it is now shown how the institutional cooperation partners of the German universities are spatially distributed. Thereby, it is demonstrated whether industry, university and research partners have become more regional or supra-regional.

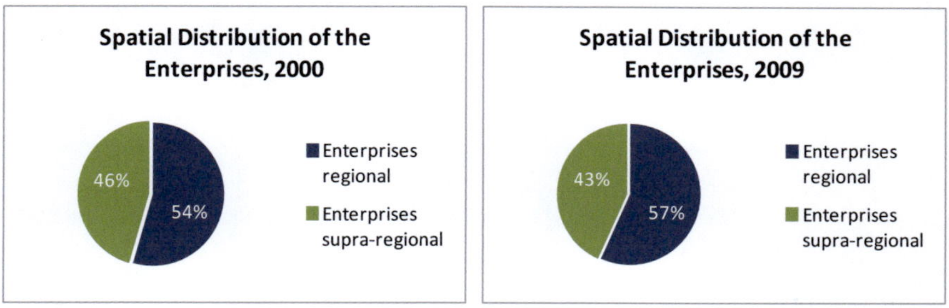

Figure 25: Spatial Distribution of the Enterprises, 2000 and 2009 (own illustration).

[62] Supra-regional located does not necessarily mean that the co-author is outside Germany.

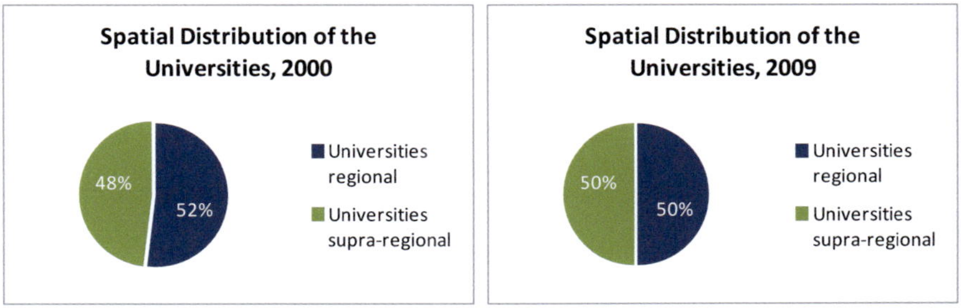

Figure 26: Spatial Distribution of the Universities, 2000 and 2009 (own illustration).

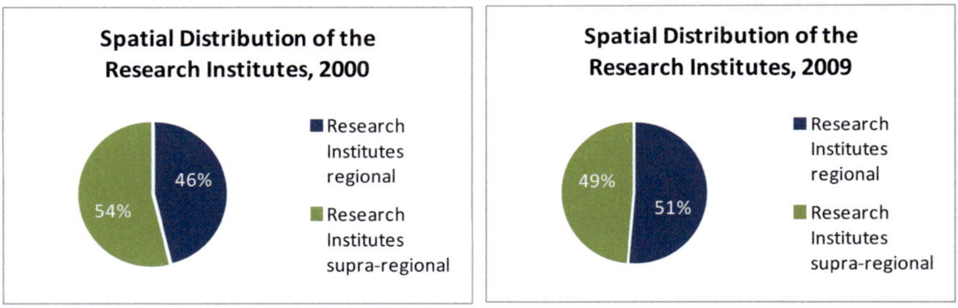

Figure 27: Spatial Distribution of the Universities, 2000 and 2009 (own illustration).

Above figures now show the spatial distribution of the different German university cooperation partners. Thereby, the spatial distribution of the enterprises from 2000 and 2009 is *firstly* presented. While the share of regionally located enterprises has been 54% in 2000, this share has even increased during the past ten years and has accounted for 57% in 2009. Thus, the German universities have started to collaborate even more often with regionally located enterprises. *Second*, coming to the spatial distribution of the universities as cooperation partners of the German universities, it can be stated that they have only hardly changed from

2000 until 2009. While the share of supra-regionally located universities has been 48% in 2000, it has been 50% in 2009; thus, universities as cooperation partners have been more or less equally distributed. *Finally*, the spatial distribution of the research institutes of the German universities from 2000 and 2009 is presented. While in 2000, the German universities have more likely cooperated with supra-regional research institutes, they meanwhile are equally engaged in regional and supra-regional network collaborations.

Overall, it can be stated that especially research and industry partners have become more regional, while the share of regional and supra-regional located universities has remained quite similar, even though the share of supra-regional located universities has become slightly higher. However, as already demonstrated, the overall distribution has shown that regional and supra-regional partners are more or less equal distributed, even though regional cooperations have generally increased in importance compared to supra-regional ones.

9. Hypotheses and Methodology concerning the three different Groups of German Universities

As already introduced in chapter four, the German universities are further classified in three different groups, which are as follows:

- Technical and non-technical universities[63]
- Medical and non-medical universities[64]
- Elite and non-elite universities[65].

This chapter now develops all relevant hypotheses regarding their collaboration behaviour for knowledge and innovation, distinguishing between the three different groups of German universities with the aim to draw differences regarding their individual behaviour. Thereby, special attention is again put on the spatial distribution of the German university co-authors with the overall aim to identify particular behavioural patterns in this regard, too.

This chapter starts with the overall question to what extent cooperation patterns differ for the German universities with different functional orientations. Thereby, the overall hypothesis is as follows:

---

[63] Further also referred to as TU and Non-TU.

[64] Further also referred to as Med and Non-Med.

[65] The elite universities are taken as they are considered to strengthen their positions within international competition. Further, they are specially promoted to also bundle research potential through networking activity. Besides, each elite university is either technical and/or medical oriented.

Hypothesis 4: *Cooperation patterns differ in case of considering the three different groups of the German universities [technical versus non-technical, medical versus non-medical and elite versus non-elite].*

First of all, it is reasonable to ask whether there are differences regarding the number of cooperations in case of the three different German university groups. In order to underpin above hypothesis theoretically, one can, for example, draw on expenditures for research and development. In this context, the following figure indicates that there are differences regarding the amount of expenditure for R&D when different fields of studies are considered:

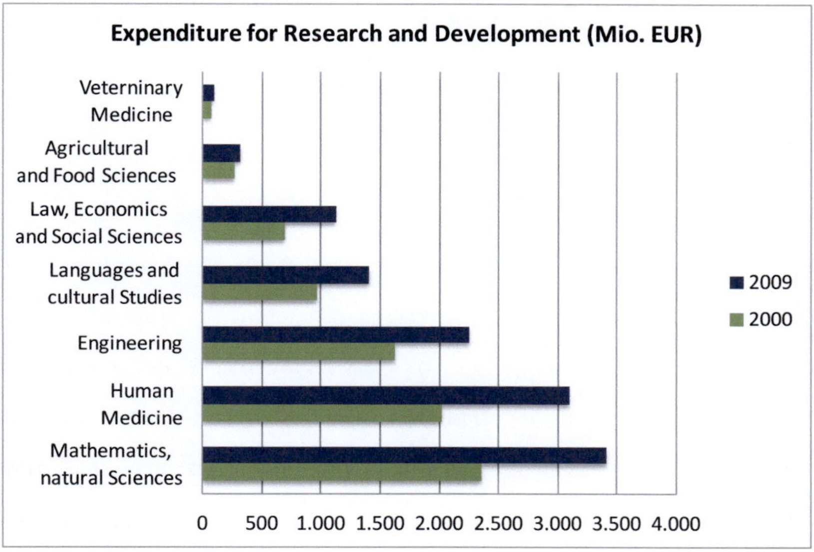

Figure 28: Expenditure for Research and Development (Mio. EUR) 2000 and 2009 (own illustration according to DESTATIS 2010).

As can be seen from the figure, while mathematics and natural sciences, human medicine and engineering have to stem high costs for research and development, it is reasonable to assume that they probably are more likely engaged in close network collaborations than the others are. Being aware of this, the following hypothesis is derived:

Hypothesis 4a: *The technical, medical and elite*[66] *universities are more engaged in close network collaborations than their counterparts due to high cost of research and pooling of resources.*

First of all, it is illustrated how far the three groups of German universities have cooperated in terms of increasing numbers of co-authored publications compared to their counterparts. Being aware of the particular distribution of single- and co-authored papers, the chi-square test is applied to explore whether there are significant differences in the distinct data sets of the three groups and their particular counterparts.

The chi-square test uses the chi-square distribution to examine whether there is a significant difference between observed frequencies and expected frequencies for the different data sets. The chi-square distribution is set up as follows:

$$\chi^2 = \sum_{i=1}^{r}\sum_{j=1}^{c}\frac{(A_{ij} - E_{ij})^2}{E_{ij}}$$

where,

A_{ij} = Actual frequency in the i'th row and j'th column

[66] The elite universities are also considered in this regard as they are either technically or medically oriented.

E_{ij} = Expected frequency in the i'th row and j'th column

r = Number of rows

c = Number of columns.

Overall, the chi-square test gives an indication of whether the value of the chi-square distribution, for independent sets of data, is likely to have occurred by chance alone. For all further conducted chi-square tests, the following null hypothesis is to be rejected: "the row variable i is independent of the column variable j". Hence, the alternative hypothesis corresponds to the variables having an association or relationship where the structure of this relationship is not specified.

For the test of independence, a chi-squared probability of less than or equal to 0.05 is commonly interpreted as justification for rejecting the null hypothesis. Thus, values of less than or equal to 0.05 are highly significant. In the course of this PhD thesis, the significance level, respectively standard errors are labeled as follows: "Standard errors: $p<0.05^*$, $p<0.01^{**}$ and $p<0.001^{***}$".

The SNA concerning the value of normalized degree centrality is further applied in order to verify and to explain the results of the chi-square test. Thus, it is proved whether possible differences are to be explained by the values of normalized degree centrality.

Further, as Powell (1990) has already stated the sources of innovative capacity are mainly found between universities, research institutes and enterprises than inside them, it is also interesting to address whether there are differences in the institutional distribution of the German university co-authors regarding the three different groups of the German universities. Literature on this topic has proposed that technical universities are more likely to cooperate with industry. Organizations as TUM-TECH GmbH which is a transfer and consulting company that helps industrial partners to get access to excellent technological and scientific knowledge of the Technical University of Munich are good examples for the increased collaborations between technical universities and industry. Further, according to Mallon (2006), research centers offer a number of benefits to academic institutions in the field of academic medicine. Further, Trune and Goslin (1996) have shown that universities with medical schools and hospitals and research centers experienced the greatest profitability overall.

Keeping in mind above consideration, the following hypothesis is formulated:

Hypothesis 4b: *The technical universities are more likely to cooperate with industrial partners due to a higher degree in applied research compared to their counterparts. In contrast, the medical universities do cooperate more often with knowledge-intensive institutions as universities and research institutes due to a higher degree in basic research-intensive bias.*

In order to shed light on the above hypothesis, a detailed institutional distribution of the German universities is shown. Hence, it is firstly pointed to possible differences within the distinct data sets of the three different groups of German universities. In order to verify the results, the chi-square test is used to illustrate whether the differences between the three groups and their counterparts are significant.

After having presented the role of the three different groups of German universities regarding their knowledge, innovation and collaboration function, the last step of the analysis refers again to proximity patterns in this regard. Thus, it is shown whether proximity patterns differ for universities with different functional orientations. As already shown before, technical universities are more likely to cooperate with industry, which in turn has become more supra-regional, so did the elite universities due to their self image as global universities. In this context, Johnson and Lybecker (2012) have found out that within the biotechnology sector knowledge is more likely to diffuse over longer distances than it was true twenty years ago. Further, following Lu and Zhao (2012), trust plays an utmost role for medical knowledge and innovation collaboration. Hence, as trust can be best built in face to face contacts, medical universities are more likely to cooperate with regional partners.

Being aware of above findings, the following hypothesis is developed:

Hypothesis 4c: *The technical and elite universities are rather engaged in collaborations with supra-regional partners compared to the non-technical and non-elite universities. The medical universities are more likely to cooperate with regional partners than the non-medical universities.*

After presenting the geographical distribution of the German university co-authors by illustrating the weights of regional and supra-regional located partners for each German university group, the chi-square test is taken to proof or disproof above hypothesis.

Up to this point, it is assumed that the elite and technical universities have rather tended to cooperate with supra-regionally located partners compared to their counterparts. In contrast, the medical universities are to be more likely engaged with regionally located partners than the non-medical universities. Besides, it has been assumed that the elite and the technical universities are more likely engaged with enterprises compared to their counterparts, while the medical universities are believed to have cooperated more often with universities and research institutes than the non-medical universities. Keeping this in mind, it is very likely that the elite and technical universities are rather engaged with supra-regional located enterprises, and the medical with regional located universities and research institutes. To shed light on this line of thought, the chi-square test is applied again. The results are displayed in the following chapter. Finally, in order to get an overview of the overall distribution of the German university co-authors according to their particular country code, it is further demonstrated how the German university co-authors are distributed regarding the five established groups of countries as introduced in *chapter six*. Literature on this topic has shown that medical- and technical-oriented research is rather found in the United States (US) or the European Union (EU) than in the emerging countries as BRIC. In this regard, is very likely that the medical, technical and elite universities are more likely to cooperate with partners coming from the United States than from emerging countries as the BRICs. After illustrating an overview of the country-based distribution of the German university co-authors, the chi-square test proves whether there are significant differences in the distinct data sets of the three groups of German universities and their counterparts.

To sum up, chapter 9 provides a detailed overview and impression of the development path of the knowledge, innovation and collaboration activity of the German universities concerning proximity patterns, always focusing on the behavioural patterns of the three different groups of German universities compared to their counterparts.

10. Empirical Results concerning the three different Groups of German Universities

Chapter ten provides a detailed overview and impression of the development path of the knowledge, innovation and collaboration activity of the German universities concerning their different functional orientation as classified before. Of course, it also highly focuses on proximity patterns and explores whether there are significant differences when the three different groups of German universities are looked at and compared with each other in this regard, too.

10.1. Publication and Cooperation Activity concerning the three different Groups of German Universities

There is no doubt that the overall publication activity of the German universities has highly increased over the past ten years. Before coming to the different behavioural patterns of the three groups of German universities regarding their collaboration activities, a nonparametric median test proves whether they possess significant differences regarding their publication activity from 2000 and from 2009. The results are as follows:

Nonparametric Median Test of Publication Activity, 2000						
	Elite	Non-Elite	Technical	Non-Technical	Medical	Non-Medical
Median	1494,5	333	553	553	972	228,5
Level of Significance	0,001***		0,95		0,001***	
Standard errors: *p≤0,05, **p≤0,01 and ***p≤0,001						

Table 16: Nonparametric Median Test of Publication Activity, 2000 (own illustration).

Nonparametric Median Test of Publication Activity, 2009						
	Elite	Non-Elite	Technical	Non-Technical	Medical	Non-Medical
Median	2572,5	691	1097	898	1708	420,5
Level of Significance	0,001***		0,538		0,001***	
Standard errors: *p≤0,05, **p≤0,01 and ***p≤0,001						

Table 17: Nonparametric Median Test of Publication Activity, 2009 (own illustration).

As can be seen from above tables, the group of elite and non-elite universities as well as the group of medical and non-medical universities possesses highly significant values regarding their medians of the publication activity. In fact, it is the elite and the medical universities that have generally published more often compared to their counterparts. This does not apply for the technical universities as they have a similar median as the non-technical universities. Hence, up to this point, it is obvious that the elite and medical universities were more likely engaged in publishing compared to the non-elite and non-medical universities.

Further, being aware of the fact that co-authorship has also highly increased over the past ten years, it is now interesting to examine whether this circumstance also differs if the three different groups of the German universities are looked at and compared with each other. In this context, it is of special interest whether there are differences within the group of technical and non-technical universities as they have not possessed a significant result regarding the median test of their publication activity. However, to statistically confirm whether there is a significant difference within the specific groups of German universities, the aforementioned chi-squared test on a fourfold table is applied. The results are as follows:

Results of the Chi-Square Test regarding the Cooperation Activity of the different Groups of German Universities, 2000-2009, P-Values				
	2000	2003	2006	2009
Elite vs. Non-Elite	0,11475	0,288640	0,239360	0,112630
TU vs. Non-TU	0,001***	0,001***	0,001***	0,001***
Med vs. Non-Med	0,001***	0,558860	0,456020	0,001***
Standard errors: *p≤0,05, **p≤0,01 and ***p≤0,001				

Table 18: Results of the Chi-Square Test regarding the Cooperation Activity of the different Groups of German Universities, 2000-2009, P-Values (own illustration).

The table illustrates the p-values of the different German university samples with regard to their cooperation activity. It is apparent that in most cases the null hypothesis can be rejected as both variables are not independent from each other. In this special case, it is proved whether cooperation activity does not depend on the specific type of German university compared to its counterpart. However, this finding does not hold in the case of the elite and non-elite universities, as they do not possess any significant differences within their data sets during the past ten years. Thus, it can be stated that the elite universities have indeed published more often as the non-elite universities, but their share of single- and co-authored publications is quite similar so that they can be neglected in this regard. In contrast, it is especially interesting to discover that the group of technical and non-technical universities possesses high significant results during all the time. Hence, they were in fact equally engaged in publishing but they have highly significant differences regarding their shares of single- and co-authored publications. Last, the medical and non-medical universities have a highly significant difference in their particular data sets within the first time period but not within the two subsequent ones. It is not until the last time period where they have again highly significant differences in their data sets regarding single- and co-authorship.

But, which type of German university is rather engaged in single-authored publications and which one is more involved in close network collaborations? The following table illustrates the share of co-authored publications of the technical and non-technical universities from 2000 until 2009:

Share of Co-authored Publications, Technical vs. Non-Technical Universities, 2000-2009				
	2000	2003	2006	2009
Technical	53%	63%	65%	68%
Non-Technical	56%	66%	69%	72%

Table 19: Share of Co-authored Publications, Technical vs. Non-Technical Universities, 2000-2009 (own illustration).

First of all, it is of course eye-catching that both groups have seen high growth rates regarding their co-authored publications. However, it is further obvious that the non-technical universities have always possessed higher rates of co-authored publications compared to the technical universities. It can be seen that in 2000, the share of the co-authored publications has been 56% for the non-technical universities compared to 53% for the technical ones. Within the last time period, the difference between single- and co-authorship has even become somewhat larger for the group of non-technical universities. Thus, while both types of universities were equally engaged in publishing, the non-technical universities have more often cooperated with others than the technical universities.

Coming now to the group of medical and non-medical universities, the following table illustrates their shares of co-authored publications from 2000 until 2009 as well:

Share of Co-authored Publications, Medical vs. Non-Medical Universities, 2000-2009				
	2000	2003	2006	2009
Medical	55%	65%	68%	71%
Non-Medical	57%	65%	68%	66%

Table 20: Share of Co-authored Publications, Medical vs. Non-Medical Universities, 2000-2009 (own illustration).

Again, as can be seen from above table, the share of co-authored publications has of course also highly increased for the medical and non-medical universities. However, in this special context, it is eye-catching that in 2000, the non-medical universities were more likely engaged in co-authored publications, while in 2009, it is the group of medical universities that has cooperated more often with other partners. Hence, the behavioural pattern in this regard has changed in favor of the medical universities within the last time period. In 2009, 71% of all publications are co-authored within the group of medical universities compared to 66% in the group of non-medical universities.

How can the changing development regarding the sample of medical and non-medical universities be properly explained? By means of the value of normalized degree centrality, it is now shown whether the medical universities have been less centralized within their knowledge networks within the first time period, and whether they could improve in this regard over the past ten years.

Nonparametric Median Test of normalised Degree Centrality, Medical vs. Non-Medical Universities, 2000 and 2009				
	2000		2009	
	Medical	Non-Medical	Medical	Non-Medical
Median	0,0233507	0,0061369	0,0327465	0,0048958
Level of Significance	0,001***		0,001***	
Standard errors: *p≤0,05, **p≤0,01 and ***p≤0,001				

Table 21: Nonparametric Median Test of normalized Degree Centrality, medical vs. non-medical universities, 2000 and 2009 (own illustration).

First of all, it is obvious that the medical universities have possessed a higher median of normalized degree centrality in both time periods even though the non-medical universities were more likely engaged in co-authored publications in 2000. But, while the median of normalized degree centrality has highly increased for the medical universities over the past ten years, it has even declined for the non-medical universities. From this, the changing development of the cooperation activity of both university types can be drawn.

To sum up, hypothesis 4a can only be partially confirmed by the findings made in this regard. It is the group of non-technical universities that have rather tended to publish in cooperation compared to their counterparts. Thus, above hypothesis is not being proved by the above findings. Further, as nowadays it is the sample of medical universities that are stronger engaged in co-authored publications, above hypothesis can at least be confirmed today in this regard.

Up to this point, it is well established that the publication and cooperation activity of the German universities has highly increased over the past ten years. Additionally, first differences regarding the particular publication and cooperation behaviour of the three different groups of the German universities could be observed, i.e. some of the German universities were generally more engaged in publishing than others, and some of them have tended to rather publish in cooperation than other did.

Further, being aware of the institutional distribution of the German university co-authors, it is now interesting to look again at the different groups of German universities, and at their individual cooperation partners. In order to statistically confirm whether there is a significant difference within the specific groups of German universities, the aforementioned chi-squared test on a fourfold table is applied. Thereby, it compares the share of private enterprises to the one of universities and research institutes as it has already been discovered that especially university-industry interactions have increased over the past years. The results are as follows:

Results of the Chi-Square Test regarding the institutional Distribution of the German University Co-Authors, 2000-2009, P-Values				
	2000	**2003**	**2006**	**2009**
Elite vs. Non-Elite	0,96656	0,98043	0,72839	0,84282
TU vs. Non-TU	0,001***	0,001***	0,001***	0,001***
Med vs. Non-Med	0,00751**	0,001***	0,001***	0,001***
Standard errors: *p≤0,05, **p≤0,01 and ***p≤0,001				

Table 22: Results of the Chi-Square Test regarding the institutional Distribution of the German University Co-Authors, 2000-2009, P-Values (own illustration).

Table 22 now illustrates that the null-hypothesis can be rejected again in most of the cases, except of the group of the elite and non-elite universities as they do not possess any differences regarding the institutional distribution of their cooperation partners. In contrast, the other two groups offer again highly significant differences regarding the institutional distribution of their co-authors. The following table shows the share of co-authorships with enterprises of the technical and non-technical universities from 2000 until 2009:

Share of Co-Authorships with Enterprises, Technical vs. Non-Technical Universities, 2000-2009				
	2000	2003	2006	2009
Technical Univeristies	8,2%	9,6%	9,7%	9,9%
Non-Techniacl Universities	5,3%	6,0%	5,5%	6,8%

Table 23: Share of Co-Authorships with Enterprises, Technical vs. Non-Technical Universities, 2000-2009 (own illustration).

Hence, according to the table, it can be proved that the technical universities have cooperated more often with enterprises than the non-technical universities. This finding holds for all four time periods. Even though the share of enterprises has only slowly increased over the past ten years regarding the technical universities, the share of enterprises has even declined from the second to the third time period regarding the non-technical universities. However, the next table now shows the share of co-authorships with enterprises of the medical and non-medical universities from 2000 until 2009:

Share of Co-Authorships with Enterprises, Medical vs. Non-Medical Universities, 2000-2009				
	2000	2003	2006	2009
Medical Universities	5,7%	6,5%	6,0%	7,2%
Non-Medical Universities	7,0%	8,2%	8,6%	9,2%

Table 24: Share of Co-Authorships with Enterprises, Medical vs. Non-Medical Universities, 2000-2009 (own illustration).

As can be seen from the table, the non-medical universities have had more linkages to enterprises over the past ten years compared to the medical universities. This finding is not surprising as it can be assumed that medical universities tend to cooperate more likely with any other knowledge-intensive institutions due to a higher degree in basic research-intensive bias. While the non-medical universities have experienced consistent increasing growth rates regarding their enterprise linkages, the medical universities have even seen declining rates of enterprise interaction from the second to the third time period.[67]

Hence, hypothesis 4b regarding the institutional distribution of the German university co-authors can be largely confirmed as the technical universities are rather engaged in close network collaborations with enterprises compared to their counterparts, and in contrast the medical universities have had more interaction to knowledge-intensive institutions than the non-medical universities. The elite and non-elite universities did not offer any differences in their cooperation behaviour with regard to the institutional distribution.

[67] The group of elite and non-elite universities has had no significant differences regarding the institutional distribution of their cooperation partners.

10.2. Innovation and Collaboration Activity concerning the three different Groups of German Universities

Coming to the innovation and collaboration activity of the three different groups of German universities, it is beyond question that they could overall increase their number of filed patents as well as their number of co-applicant networks. However, it is still questionable whether all German universities have developed equally in this regard. Hence, by means of the value of betweenness centrality, it is shown whether there are differences regarding close network collaborations between the three different groups of German universities. The results are as follows:

Nonparametric Median Test of Betweenness Centrality, Co-Applicant Networks, 2007-2008						
	Elite	Non-Elite	Technical	Non-Technical	Medical	Non-Medical
Median	0,0240416	0	0,00551905	0	0,0073643	0
Level of Significance	0,003**		0,107		0,011**	
Standard errors: *p≤0,05, **p≤0,01 and ***p≤0,001						

Table 25: Nonparametric Median Test of Betweenness Centrality, Co-Applicant Networks, 2007-2008 (own illustration).

It can be observed that all counterpart universities have a median of zero regarding the median of betweenness centrality. First of all, it has to be stated that the overall patenting activity of the German universities is still comparably low. Second, the differences regarding the median of betweenness centrality between the three different groups of German universities have only been significant in the case of elite and non-elite universities as well as in the case of medical and non-medical universities. Hence, the elite and the medical universities have been more important as central links within the innovation networks compared to their counterparts. Overall, hypothesis 4a is confirmed for the elite and medical universities, but needs to be rejected for the technical universities.

Further, as it has been done for the publication data, it is also proved for the patent applications whether there are significant differences in the distribution of their cooperation partners when the different groups of German universities are explored and compared with each other. Before coming to the results of the chi-square test, the following figure firstly refers to the distribution of the distinct cooperation partners of the elite, technical and medical universities in order to provide an overview in this regard:

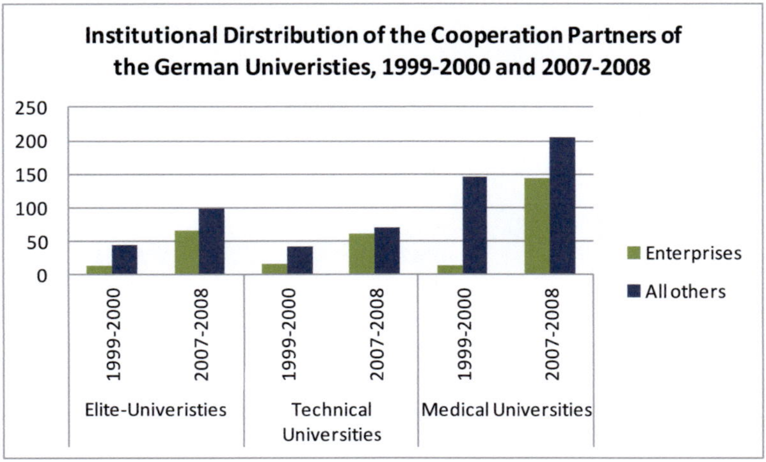

Figure 29: Institutional Distribution of the Cooperation Partners of the German Universities, absolute numbers, 1999-2000 and 2007-2008 (own illustration).

As each group of German universities consists of a different number of universities, it is of course not reasonable to compare the absolute numbers of cooperation partners of the three different German university groups. But, it is of interest to have a look at the development of the number of partnerships, either to enterprises or to all others, of each single group itself. Hence, it is obvious that the increase of private enterprises is very strong in each group, and always much stronger than the rise of all other institutional partners. While the elite universities could increase their partnerships with private enterprises by 400%, and the technical universities by around 250%, it is striking that the medical universities have experienced the largest increase of private enterprises as institutional partners which amounts to 1,000%. But, in comparison to all other cooperation partners, it is the elite and technical universities that have more likely cooperated with enterprises. The rise of all other partners is relative similar in each of the three groups and ranges from 40% up to 125%. Nonetheless, private enterprises seem to require more academic knowledge which is expressed through the number of partnerships.

In the following, the results of the chi-square test are illustrated for the three different German university samples; thus, it is statistically shown whether there are significant differences in the distribution of their cooperation partners. The test is done for the first, third and fifth time period. The results are as follows:

Results of the Chi-Square Test regarding the institutional Distribution of the German University Co-Applicants, P-Values of three Time Periods			
	1999-2000	2003-2004	2007-2008
Elite vs. Non-Elite	0,02521**	0,18004	0,86869
TU vs. Non-TU	0,001***	0,18457	0,10432
Med vs. Non-Med	0,001***	0,80868	0,48959
Standard errors: *p≤0,05, **p≤0,01 and ***p≤0,001			

Table 26: Results of the Chi-Square Test regarding the institutional Distribution of the German University Co-Applicants, P-Values of three Time Periods (own illustration).

While the table shows highly significant values for each German university sample within the first time period, this finding cannot be confirmed within the last time period. However, in order to explore which groups of the German universities have rather tended to cooperate with enterprises compared to their counterparts, the following figure shows the absolute numbers of co-applicants of each German university group:

Institutional Distribution of the German University Co-Applicants, 1999-2000 and 2007-2008						
1999-2000	Elite	Non-Elite	Technical	Non-Technical	Medical	Non-Medical
Enterprises	13	15	17	14	13	18
All others	43	124	41	137	146	32
Share Enterprises (%)	23	12	29	9	8	36
2007-2008	Elite	Non-Elite	Technical	Non-Technical	Medical	Non-Medical
Enterprises	65	122	60	129	144	43
All others	98	178	70	211	204	71
Share Enterprises (%)	40	41	46	38	41	38

Table 27: Institutional Distribution of the German University Co-Applicants, absolute numbers, 1999-2000 and 2007-2008 (own illustration).

Figure 28 indicates that there are significant differences within the three German university samples for the first time period. Thus, it is interesting to show which group of German universities has rather tended to cooperate with enterprises or with other institutional partners[68]. It is illustrated how all groups behave regarding their co-applicants. In the group of elite universities, around 23% of all co-applicants were among the enterprises compared to only 12% within the group of the non-elite universities. Thus, from 1999 until 2001, the German elite universities have rather cooperated with enterprises than the non-elite universities. However, this finding has changed over time, as during the last time period, the share of the enterprises has been similar in both groups. This finding also holds for the group of medical

[68] In this context, other institutional partners include other universities, research institutes and private persons.

and non-medical universities. While within the first time period, the share of enterprises was 36% in the group of non-medical universities, compared to only 8% within the other group of medical universities, the share of enterprises as co-applicants is nowadays quite similar in both groups. Thus, it is obvious that especially the medical universities have started to cooperate with enterprises. Besides, the examination of the technical and non-technical universities looks a bit different, as there are still slight significant differences in both samples regarding the share of enterprises as institutional co-applicants. In the first time period, cooperations of the technical universities with enterprises have accounted for around 30%, while the share of enterprises within the group of non-technical universities has only been 9%. Nowadays, the share of private enterprises has highly increased within the group of non-technical enterprises, too. Overall, hypothesis 4b is largely confirmed in terms of patents by above findings.

10.3. Proximity Patterns concerning the three different Groups of German Universities

This subchapter now highlights proximity patterns concerning again the three different groups of German universities, in order to prove whether the elite, technical or medical universities are more likely to cooperate with supra-regional partners compared to their counterparts or the other way round. Thereby, it is firstly looked at the distribution of the

German university co-authors based on their geographical coordinates. Afterwards, it is illustrated how they are linked to others based on country codes.

However, being aware of the fact that supra-regional cooperation partners are at least as important as regionally located partners, it is further highly interesting to examine which groups of the German universities tend to rather cooperate with partners that are supra-regionally located or not. Thus, in the following, it is proved whether there are significant differences regarding the spatial distribution when the three different German university groups are examined and compared with each other.

The following figure firstly presents an overview of the development of the co-authors of the elite, technical, and medical German universities for 2000 and 2009[69].

[69] It is again not reasonable to compare the absolute numbers of the regional and supra-regional located co-authors of each group as they are of different size. Thus, it is interesting to compare how the relation of regionally located to supra-regionally located co-authors has developed over the past ten years.

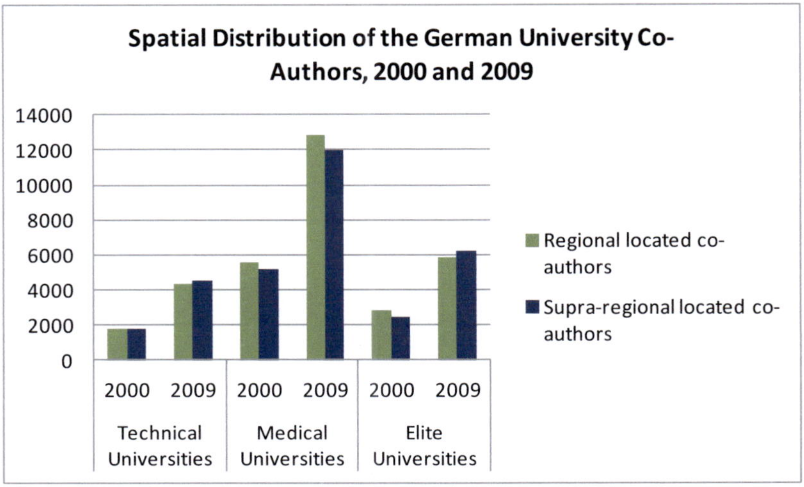

Figure 30: Spatial Distribution of the German University Co-Authors, 2000 and 2009 (own illustration).

It is apparent that within the first time period, the share of regionally located co-authors is always higher than the share of supra-regionally located ones. But, over the past years, this finding has partially turned to the opposite as in 2009 the share of supra-regionally located co-authors is slightly higher regarding the technical and elite universities. But, the medical universities are still more likely to cooperate with regionally located co-authors as above figure illustrates. While regionally located co-authors have increased by around 130% on average from 2000 until 2009, the rise of supra-regionally located co-authors has amounted to around 140% on average during the same time period.

The following table now illustrates the p-values of the three different groups of German universities regarding the spatial distribution of their cooperation partners. Thereby, it has been proved if the variables proximity and type of German university are independent from each other or not. The results are as follows:

Results of the Chi-Square Test regarding the spatial Distribution of the German University Co-Authors, 2000-2009 (P-Values)				
	2000	2003	2006	2009
Elite vs. Non-Elite	0,7831	0,001***	0,001***	0,001***
TU vs. Non-TU	0,001***	0,001***	0,001***	0,001***
Med vs. Non-Med	0,001***	0,001***	0,001***	0,001***
Standard errors: *p≤0,05, **p≤0,01 and ***p≤0,001				

Table 28: P-Values of different German University-Samples, regional versus non-regional Activities, 2000-2009 (own illustration).

As can be seen from the table, the null-hypothesis can be rejected in almost all cases, thus, the German university groups behave differently regarding the spatial distribution of their particular co-authors. It is only the group of elite versus non-elite universities that did not offer any significant results within the first time period. However, it is now interesting to explore which group has tended to cooperate more with supra-regionally located partners.

The following figure now firstly refers to the spatial distribution of the cooperation partners of the elite and non-elite universities from 2000 and 2009:

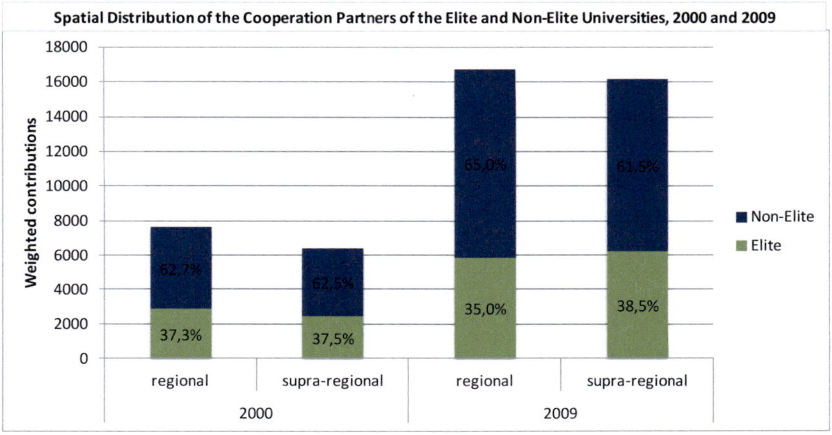

Figure 31: Spatial Distribution of the Cooperation Partners of the elite and non-elite universities from 2000 and 2009, weighted Numbers (own illustration).

As can be seen from the figure, while there are no significant differences between the elite and non-elite universities regarding the spatial distribution of their cooperation partners in 2000, the bars of the last time period illustrate that the elite universities are more likely to cooperate with supra-regionally located partners compared to the non-elite universities. In 2009, 38.5% of the cooperation partners of the elite universities were supra-regional located compared to smaller share (35.0%) that were regional located. The distribution of cooperation partners of the non-elite universities was the other way round. While 61.5% were supra-regionally located, a higher proportion (65.0%) was regional. Hence, above derived hypothesis in this regard can be confirmed for the elite universities.

The following figure shows the spatial distribution of the cooperation partners of the technical and non-technical universities in order to clarify the above results of the chi-square test:

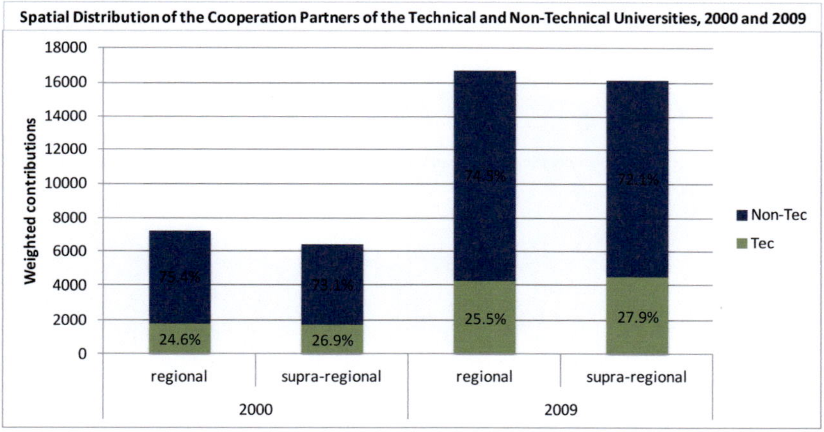

Figure 32: Spatial Distribution of the Cooperation Partners of the Technical and Non-Technical Universities, 2000 and 2009, weighted Numbers (own illustration).

The technical and non-technical universities have offered significant differences regarding the spatial distribution of their cooperation partners in all time periods. Within the first one, it can be seen from the figure that the share of the regional located co-authors of the technical universities was smaller, and the proportion of the supra-regionally located ones was larger compared to the non-technical universities. The same finding holds for the last time period. Thus, above hypothesis can be also confirmed for the technical universities as they were more likely to cooperate with supra-regionally located partners compared to their counterparts.

Finally, the next table provides information on the spatial distribution of the co-authors of the medical and non-medical universities for 2000 and 2009:

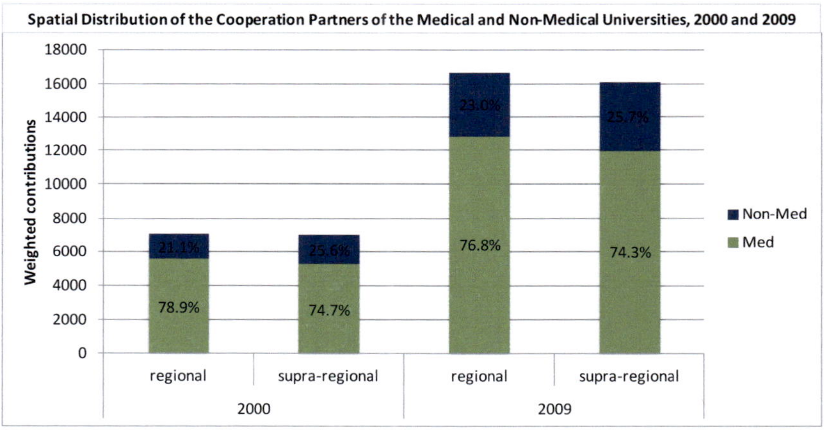

Figure 33: Spatial Distribution of the Cooperation Partners of the Medical and Non-Medical Universities, 2000 and 2009, weighted Numbers (own illustration).

As it holds for the group of technical and non-technical universities, the medical and non-medical ones have also possessed highly significant differences regarding the spatial distribution of their cooperation partners during all the time of assessment. In contrast to the other two groups of German universities, the medical universities were more likely to cooperate with regionally located partners compared to the non-medical universities. This finding counts for both time periods. Thus, the findings of this PhD thesis also confirm the hypothesis that due to the important role of trust in medical knowledge collaborations, proximity patterns still highly matter.

Up to this point, it is well known that the elite and the technical universities have rather tended to cooperate with supra-regionally located partners compared to their counterparts. In contrast, the medical universities have been more likely to cooperate with regionally located partners than the non-medical universities. Hence, hypothesis 4c is entirely confirmed by above findings. Further, as already discussed, the share of supra-regionally located universities could have been increased most, while the share of supra-regionally located enterprises and research institutes has even decreased over the past ten years. Last, it is also known that the technical universities have more likely cooperated with enterprises and the medical universities have been more engaged with research institutes.

Keeping this in mind, it is very likely that the elite and technical universities have been rather engaged with supra-regionally located enterprises, and the medical with regionally located research institutes and universities. Hence, it is further examined which institutional cooperation partners have been rather regionally or supra-regionally located concerning again the different functional orientation of the German universities. In order to shed light on this line of thought, the chi-square test is applied again. The test has been made three times, for the enterprises, for the research institutes as well as for the universities.

The next table refers to all interactions with enterprises. The results are as follows:

Results of the Chi-Square Test regarding the spatial Distribution of the Enterprises, 2000-2009, P-Values				
	2000	**2003**	**2006**	**2009**
Elite vs. Non-Elite	0,18176	0,00677**	0,24178	0,0562*
TU vs. Non-TU	0,74948	0,69506	0,00415**	0,03148*
Med vs. Non-Med	0,01272**	0,27837	0,16645	0,05445*
Standard errors: *p≤0,05, **p≤0,01 and ***p≤0,001				

Table 29: Results of the Chi-Square Test regarding the spatial Distribution of the Enterprises, 2000-2009, P-Values (own illustration).

First of all, the results of the spatial distribution of the enterprises are displayed. As can be seen from the table, there are no consistent significant results. The group of elite and non-elite universities has possessed differences in their particular distributions in 2003 and in 2009, the group of technical and non-technical universities within the last two time periods, and finally, the group of medical and non-medical within the first and within the last time period. However, in 2003 and 2009, the elite universities have cooperated more often with supra-regionally located enterprises compared to their counterparts. Hence, while the elite and non-elite universities have not offered any significant results regarding the overall distribution of their cooperation partners, the elite universities have been indeed more engaged with supra-regionally located enterprises than the non-elite universities. In 2006 and 2009, it has been the non-technical universities that have rather cooperated with supra-regionally located enterprises. Thus, above hypothesis has to be rejected in this regard. The technical universities have been more engaged with enterprises and with supra-regionally located cooperation partners, but not with supra-regionally located enterprises. Finally, in 2000 and 2009, the non-medical universities have tended to rather publish with supra-regionally located enterprises compared to the medical universities, even though the difference has become smaller. Thus, above drawn hypothesis can be confirmed in this regard.

Further, the following table shows the results of the chi-square test regarding the spatial distribution of the research institutes from 2000 until 2009.

Results of the Chi-Square Test regarding the spatial Distribution of the Research Institutes, 2000-2009, P-Values				
	2000	**2003**	**2006**	**2009**
Elite vs. Non-Elite	0,12035	0,56401	0,48587	0,49741
TU vs. Non-TU	0,09906	0,001***	0,001**	0,91921
Med vs. Non-Med	0,001***	0,04826*	0,001***	0,00873**
Standard errors: *p≤0,05, **p≤0,01 and ***p≤0,001				

Table 30: Results of the Chi-Square Test regarding the spatial Distribution of the Research Institutes, 2000-2009, P-Values (own illustration).

At the first glance, it is obvious that the elite and non-elite universities have never possessed any differences in their spatial cooperation manner with regard to the research institutes. But as they have not possessed any significant differences regarding the overall distribution of their cooperation partners, the finding is not too surprising in this regard. Besides, the results of the chi-square test of the technical and non-technical universities are highly significant in 2003 and 2006, and the group of medical and non-medical universities has had consequently significant results regarding their particular cooperation behaviour. In 2003 and 2006, the technical universities have cooperated more often with supra-regionally located research institutes than the non-technical universities, even though the overall share of the supra-regionally located research institutes has highly decreased from 2003 until 2006. Even though the technical universities have been overall more engaged in collaborations with enterprises, they have been more likely to cooperate with supra-regionally located research institutes compared to the non-technical universities. Finally, it has been the medical universities that have rather cooperated with regionally located research institutes. Thus, above hypothesis can be confirmed in this regard. The medical universities have not only been more engaged with regionally located partners, they were also more likely to cooperate with regionally located research institutes.

The last table illustrates the results of the chi-square test according to the spatial distribution of the universities from 2000 until 2009.

Results of the Chi-Square Test regarding the spatial Distribution of the Universities, 2000-2009, P-Values				
	2000	**2003**	**2006**	**2009**
Elite vs. Non-Elite	0,11752	0,001***	0,001***	0,001***
TU vs. Non-TU	0,001***	0,001***	0,001***	0,001***
Med vs. Non-Med	0,001***	0,001***	0,001***	0,001***
Standard errors: *p≤0,05, **p≤0,01 and ***p≤0,001				

Table 31: Results of the Chi-Square Test regarding the spatial Distribution of the Universities, 2000-2009, P-Values (own illustration).

It is very apparent that almost all results have been highly significant regarding the spatial distribution of the universities. Thereby, the elite universities have cooperated more often with supra-regionally located universities compared to the non-elite universities. Further, the technical universities have had more linkages to supra-regionally located universities than the non-technical universities. Thus, above derived hypothesis has to be rejected in this regard. Last, the medical universities have cooperated more often with regionally located universities than the non-medical universities so that the hypothesis is to be confirmed.

Up to this point, it is well known where about the German university co-authors are located. Further, it has also been shown how the German university cooperation partners have been institutionally located. Thereby, all explorations have been done for the three different German university groups in order to demonstrate differences in their particular cooperation behaviour. But, in this context, it is only differentiated whether they are regionally or supra-regionally located; thus, information on the exact localisation of the German university co-authors is still missing. In the following, the geographical distribution of the German university co-authors depending on where they are coming from is presented; thus, it is a country-based analysis.

However, before coming to the three different groups of German universities, the following figure firstly shows the overall distribution of the German university co-authors according to their country codes. Thereby, due to the fact that the co-authors have come from around 140 different countries, six different groups have been developed as described in *chapter six*.

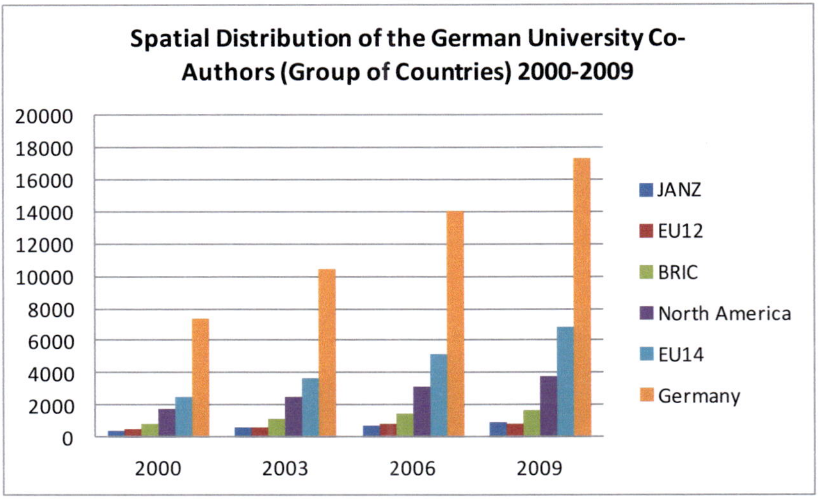

Figure 34: Spatial Distribution of the German University Co-Authors (Groups of Countries), weighted Numbers, 2000-2009 (own illustration).

As can be seen from the figure, each group has experienced high growth rates regarding their linkages to the German universities. It can be observed that the group of Germany is especially strong during all time periods, followed by the group of EU14 and North America. Besides, the number of cooperations to the other three groups of countries is still comparable low. However, the strongest increase of cooperations from 2000 until 2009 can be found within the group of the EU14 followed by Germany and JANZ. North America has occupied fourth place, BRIC fifth place, and finally, the EU12 sixth place regarding the increase of linkages to the German universities. The countries of the EU12 can rather be neglected as they even occupy last place in 2009, even though the group includes much more countries compared to the groups of JANZ and BRIC, and furthermore, they are much more closer located to the German universities. Thus, the groups of the EU14, North America, JANZ as well as the emergent countries of BRIC remain to be explored in more detail. First of all, it is shown whether the elite and non-elite, the technical and non-technical as well as the medical and non-medical German universities have rather cooperated with partners coming from North America or from EU14. A second step further proves if the three different groups of German universities have more likely cooperated with partners coming from North America, or with partners coming from BRIC or JANZ. The same analysis is further done for EU14 compared to BRIC and JANZ, too. The chi-square test is again used to observe possible differences in the particular distributions of the three different German university groups. All tests are conducted for the first and the last time period.

The following table now shows if there are significant differences among the three groups of German universities regarding their linkages to cooperation partners coming from North America compared to those coming from EU14.

Results of the Chi-Square Test regarding the spatial Distribution, North America vs. EU14, 2000 and 2009, P-Values		
	2000	**2009**
Elite vs. Non-Elite	0,83582	0,37861
TU vs. Non-TU	0,00866**	0,52326
Med vs. Non-Med	0,03038*	0,00441**
Standard errors: *p≤0,05, **p≤0,01 and ***p≤0,001		

Table 32: Results of the Chi-Square Test regarding the spatial Distribution, North America vs. EU14, 2000 and 2009, P-Values (own illustration).

While the group of elite and non-elite universities does not possess any significant results in this regard, the technical and non-technical universities have at least a significant result in 2000 and the medical and non-medical universities even in both time periods. Thereby, the technical universities have rather cooperated with partners coming from the EU14 compared to the non-technical universities, and the medical universities have more likely cooperated with partners from North America compared to their counterparts.

However, the following table illustrates the results of the chi-square test regarding the spatial distribution between the occurrence of co-authors coming from North America compared to BRIC and JANZ for each group for 2000 and 2009:

Results of the Chi-Square Test regarding the spatial Distribution, North America vs. BRIC & North America vs. JANZ, 2000 and 2009, P-Values				
	North America vs. BRIC		North America vs. JANZ	
	2000	2009	2000	2009
Elite vs. Non-Elite	0,001***	0,001***	0,61871	0,73268
TU vs. Non-TU	0,001***	0,001***	0,01566**	0,001***
Med vs. Non-Med	0,001***	0,001***	0,10803	0,03435*
Standard errors: *p≤0,05, **p≤0,01 and ***p≤0,001				

Table 33: Results of the Chi-Square Test regarding the spatial Distribution, USA vs. BRIC & USA vs. Janz, 2000 and 2009, P-Values (own illustration).

As can be seen from the table, the results of the chi-square test regarding the spatial distribution of the German university co-authors, either being in North America located or in BRIC, are for each group and for both years highly significant. Thereby, the elite universities have had more cooperation partners from North America, the technical universities have more often cooperated with partners from BRIC, and finally, the medical universities have had also more linkages to North American partners compared to their counterparts. These findings hold for both time periods. Regarding the collaborations with partners from North America compared to those coming from JANZ, the group of elite and non-elite universities does not offer any significant results. The technical and non-technical universities have differences in their data sets in both time periods, and the medical and non-medical universities show differences at least within the last time period. It is the group of technical universities which has rather cooperated with partners coming from JANZ compared to the non-technical universities, and it is the medical universities that have had also more linkages to North America than the non-medical universities.

Finally, the following table shows the results of the chi-square test regarding the spatial distribution of co-authors coming from the EU14 compared to co-authors coming from BRIC and from JANZ for 2000 and 2009:

Results of the Chi-Square Test regarding the spatial Distribution, EU14 vs. BRIC & EU14 vs. JANZ, 2000 and 2009, P-Values				
	EU14 vs. BRIC		EU14 vs. JANZ	
	2000	2009	2000	2009
Elite vs. Non-Elite	0,001***	0,001***	0,61871	0,88805
TU vs. Non-TU	0,001***	0,001***	0,34899	0,001***
Med vs. Non-Med	0,001***	0,001***	0,69745	0,57447
Standard errors: *p≤0,05, **p≤0,01 and ***p≤0,001				

Table 34: Results of the Chi-Square Test regarding the spatial distribution, EU14 vs. BRIC & EU14 vs. JANZ, 2000 and 2009, P-Values (own illustration).

Again, the results of the chi-square test regarding the spatial distribution of the German university co-authors coming from the EU14 compared to those who are coming from BRIC are highly significant for each group and for both years. In this context, the elite universities have had more cooperation partners which have come from the EU14, the technical universities have more often cooperated with partners from BRIC, and finally, the medical universities have had also more linkages to the

European partners. These findings hold for both time periods. Regarding the cooperations with partners from the EU14 compared to those coming from JANZ, the groups of elite and non-elite as well as the medical and non-medical universities did not offer any significant results. It is only the group of technical and non-technical universities that have had significant differences in their particular data sets regarding the spatial distribution of their co-authors. Within the last time period, the technical universities have cooperated more often with partners coming from JANZ than from EU14 compared to the non-technical universities.

To sum up, the elite and non-elite universities possess less significant values regarding the spatial distribution of their cooperation partners depending on where they are coming from. However, the elite universities have been more likely linked to partners coming from North America and EU14 than from BRIC. In contrast, the technical and non-technical as well as the medical and non-medical universities have frequently occurring significant values in this regard. The technical universities have cooperated more often with partners coming BRIC and JANZ than from North America and EU14 compared their counterparts, while the medical universities have had more likely linkages to partners from North America and EU14 than from BRIC and JANZ compared to the non-medical universities.

These important findings will be further discussed within the last chapter regarding the final conclusion, reflection and policy recommendations.

11. The Cases of the Karlsruhe Institute of Technology and the University of Heidelberg

This last part of empirical analysis is based upon two German elite universities, namely the Karlsruhe Institute of Technology (KIT) and the University of Heidelberg. Thereby, the KIT is a technical and former elite university, while the University of Heidelberg is a medical and an elite one. These two universities have been selected as most differences have been found between the samples of technical/elite universities and the sample of medical universities. They show differences not only in their overall publication, patenting and collaboration behaviour, but also with regard to the institutional and spatial distribution of their cooperation partners. Thus, it is reasonable to compare two elite universities, whereas one is technically-focused and the other one is medical.[70]

In the following, all relevant former analyses are conducted solely for both chosen universities in order to compare them with each other, and to identify special behavioural patterns for each type of university. First of all, the next figure shows the overall publication and cooperation activity of the KIT and the University of Heidelberg[71].

[70] Both universities are further taken as they are under the best-performers regarding their publication, patenting and cooperation activity.
[71] In the following course of this chapter referred to as solely Heidelberg.

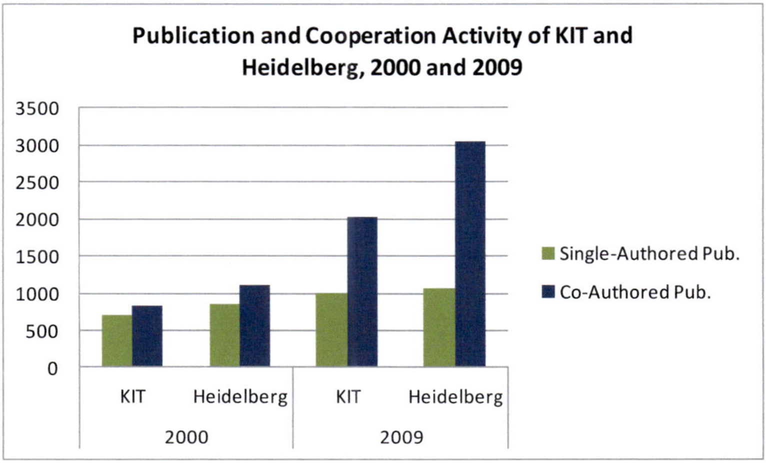

Figure 35: Publication and Cooperation Activity of KIT and Heidelberg, absolute Numbers, 2000 and 2009 (own illustration).

In the first instance, it can be seen that the overall publication activity of Heidelberg is higher than the one of the KIT. But, it should be mentioned in this regard that in 2008 the KIT has possessed around 240 professors and 18,000 students compared to around 280 professors and 25,000 students in Heidelberg. Hence, in the following analysis, it has to be kept in mind that it is not surprising to have some differences in size regarding their overall publication and cooperation activity.

Overall, the KIT has increased its number of publications by about 100%, while Heidelberg could even raise their publications by 110%. Regarding the share of co-authored publications, 54% of the overall publications have been co-authored at the KIT in 2000, and around 56% in Heidelberg. Thus, both universities did not yet show big differences regarding their publication and cooperation behaviour. Later on, they could even enlarge their shares of co-authored publication; the KIT has increased its share of co-authored publications by 140%, and Heidelberg by even 170%. Hence, Heidelberg is a bit more engaged in co-authored publications than the KIT which is not surprising as the analysis of all German universities has shown that the technical universities have been less engaged in co-authored publications compared to the non-technical universities, while the medical universities have more likely cooperated with other partners compared to their counterparts.

Keeping in mind that both universities are extremely involved in close network collaborations as the highly increasing number of co-authored publications indicates, the following figure shows the absolute numbers of co-authors, as well as the values of degree and betweenness centrality, whereas degree centrality points to the distinct number of co-authors and betweenness centrality to the importance of the particular university as knowledge intermediary within the network as already discussed above.

Absolute Number of Co-Authors, Degree and Betweenness Centrality, KIT and Heidelberg, 2000 & 2009				
	2000		2009	
	KIT	Heidelberg	KIT	Heidelberg
Absolute No of Co-Authors	4460	7261	11643	19695
Normalized Degree Centrality	0,0555385	0,0643142	0,0525349	0,091701
Betweenness Centrality	0,0757067	0,0854576	0,062739	0,097603

Table 35: Absolute Number of Co-Authors, Degree and Betweenness Centrality of KIT and Heidelberg, 2000 and 2009 (own illustration).

Above table shows that in 2000, the KIT has possessed 4,460 cooperation partners and Heidelberg even 7,261. During the past years, the KIT could increase its number of co-authors by around 150%, and Heidelberg by approximately 180%. Regarding the value of normalized degree centrality which can be for example used to compare networks of different size, it is obvious that Heidelberg has had a much higher value than the KIT, especially with regard to the last time period. Further, while Heidelberg could even highly raise its value of normalized degree centrality, the KIT has even lost strength in this regard. The same finding holds for the value of betweenness centrality as Heidelberg could again improve itself over the past ten years, becoming more central within the knowledge networks, while the value of betweenness centrality of the KIT has dropped from 0,0757067 in 2000 down to 0,062739 in 2009. Hence, Heidelberg has been more involved in close network collaborations over the past ten years and has been more important as knowledge intermediary within the knowledge networks compared to the KIT. Remembering above finding that the average mean value of betweenness centrality has decreased over the past ten years, it has been demonstrated that, amongst other, the KIT is one of the universities that have had decreasing values in this regard.

Coming to the institutional distribution of the co-authors of the KIT and Heidelberg, the following figure illustrates to what extent the two universities have been linked to either other universities, research institutes, enterprises or to the subject of study itself.

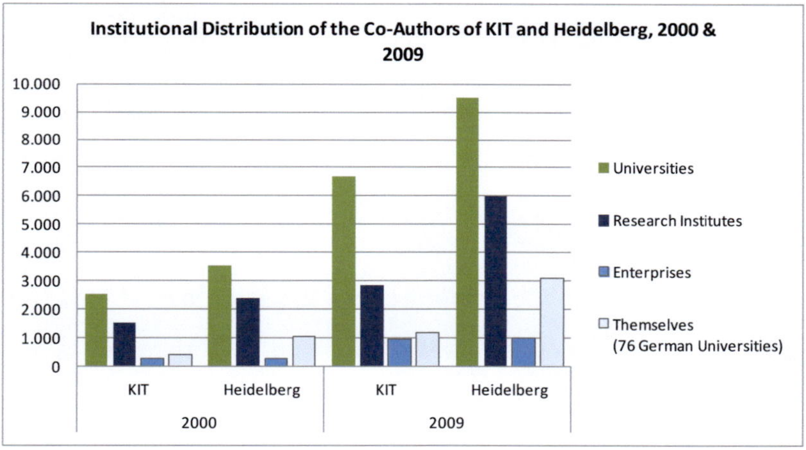

Figure 36: Institutional Distribution of the Co-Authors of KIT and Heidelberg, absolute Numbers, 2000 and 2009 (own illustration).

As can be seen from above figure, the highest share of cooperation partners has been allocated to the universities followed by the research institutes, the German universities themselves and finally the enterprises. But how about comparing the shares of each cooperation partner of the KIT and Heidelberg? For doing this, the following table illustrates the particular shares of the co-authors of both universities:

Particular Share of the institutional Co-Authors, KIT and Heidelberg, 2000 and 2009 (%)				
	2000		2009	
	KIT	Heidelberg	KIT	Heidelberg
Other Univeristies	54	48	57	48
Research Institutes	32	33	25	31
Enterprises	5	3	8	5
Themselves (76 German Universities)	8	14	10	16

Table 36: Percentage Share of the different Co-Authors of KIT and Heidelberg, 2000 and 2009 (own illustration).

First of all, the table demonstrates that the percentage share of the other universities and the enterprises has increased over the past ten years. While the group of research institutes has remained almost similar in the case of Heidelberg, it has highly declined in the case of the KIT. Last, the 76 German universities as potential cooperation partners have become more important for the KIT as well as for Heidelberg. However, it is obvious that the KIT has been more involved in close network collaborations with enterprises compared to Heidelberg, and Heidelberg has more likely cooperated with research institutes than the KIT. Hence, the result of the chi-square test in this regard for all technical and medical universities can be confirmed by above finding, too.

Being aware of the institutional distribution of the co-authors of the KIT and Heidelberg, the next step considers distance patterns. Thus, the following figure firstly shows the spatial distribution of the co-authors of the KIT and Heidelberg within the 1,000 km radius from 2009:

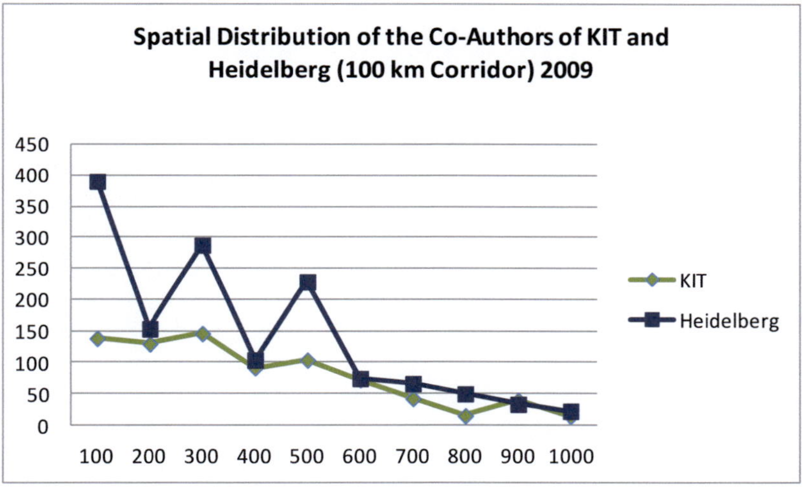

Figure 37: Spatial Distribution of the Co-Authors of KIT and Heidelberg (100 km Corridor) weighted Numbers, 2009 (own illustration).

As can be seen from the figure, the spatial distribution of the co-authors of the KIT and Heidelberg has differed greatly. While Heidelberg has been highly engaged in local network collaborations, the spatial distribution of the cooperation partners of the KIT is more consistent as it shows a slowly declining trend with the growth of distance. This finding does not hold for Heidelberg, at least for the first 500 km, as the spatial distribution of its co-authors is highly differing. From around 500 km onwards, Heidelberg has also experienced a decreased number of cooperation partners with the growth of distance. Hence, above figure already indicates that Heidelberg as medical oriented university seems to be more likely engaged with local cooperation partners compared to the KIT as technical oriented university. Thus, locality might be especially important for medical universities than for the technical universities.

However, to perceive a more valid impression in this regard, the following figure firstly shows the spatial distribution of all cooperation partners for 2000 and 2009, either being regionally or supra-regionally located:

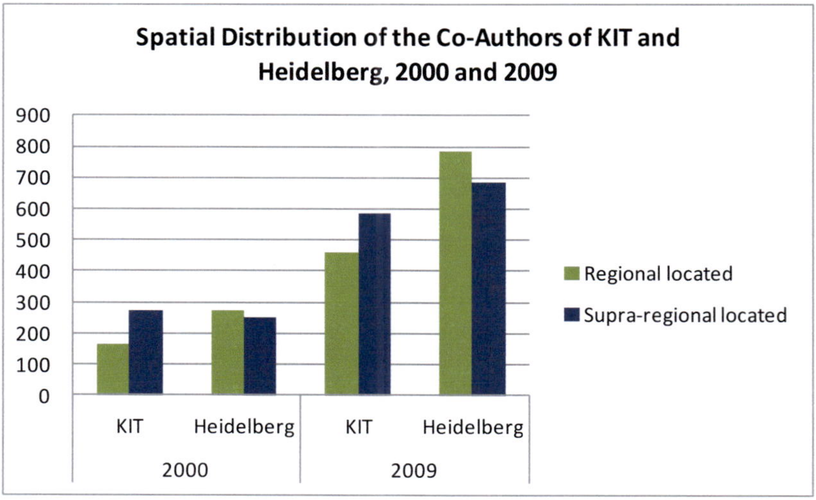

Figure 38: Spatial Distribution of the Co-Authors, KIT and Heidelberg, absolute Numbers, 2000 and 2009 (own illustration).

As it has already been presented through the overall illustration of the spatial distribution of the German university co-authors, the KIT as technical university has always possessed more linkages to supra-regional cooperation partners, while Heidelberg as medical university has more likely cooperated with regional located cooperation partners over the past ten years. In 2000, the KIT has possessed around 63% cooperation partners which has been supra-regional located, while in 2009 this percentage share has decreased by six percentage points. However, the KIT is still more engaged in supra-regional collaborations. In contrast, Heidelberg has possessed around 52% co-authors which has been regional located in 2000 and has even increased this percentage share by two percentage points. Heidelberg has more likely cooperated with regionally located cooperation partners. Hence, above hypothesis considering all German universities can be also confirmed by this finding.

In order to better estimate which cooperation partners have been regionally located and which ones have been more likely supra-regionally located, the following figure firstly shows the regional distribution of the co-authors of the KIT and Heidelberg for 2000 and 2009:

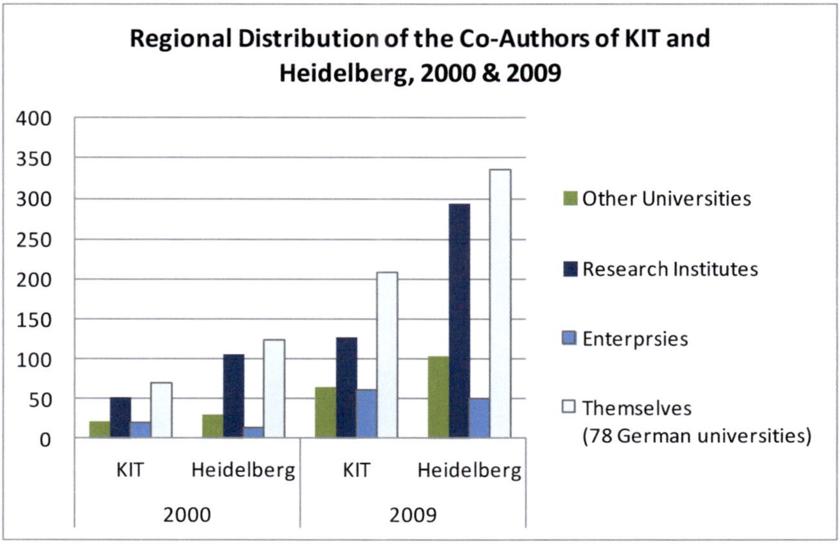

Figure 39: Regional Distribution of the Co-Authors of KIT and Heidelberg, weighted Numbers, 2000 and 2009 (own illustration).

It can be seen that the regional distribution of the co-authors of the KIT and Heidelberg somewhat differs. Within the first time period, most of the cooperation partners of the KIT have come from the German universities themselves followed by research institutes. The other universities and the enterprises have shared third place in 2000. Referring to the distribution of the cooperation partners of Heidelberg, it is the group of German universities that have been at the fore front closely followed by the research institutes, too. With a considerably lower share, the other universities and the enterprises have been followed. Overall, it is the KIT that has been much more engaged in close network collaborations with regionally located enterprises, and it is Heidelberg that have more likely cooperated with regionally located research institutes. However, it is also obvious that within the regional distribution of the co-authors of the KIT and Heidelberg, the share of the German universities themselves has highly increased over the past ten years. Thus, both have been frequently engaged in close network collaborations with themselves (76 German universities)[72], while the share of the other universities as well as the share of the research institutes has declined.

Ten years later, all shares have only slightly changed. In the case of the KIT, it is the German universities and the enterprises which have been increased, while the group of research institutes as well as the group of other universities have become lower. For Heidelberg, it is also the group of German universities and enterprises which have increased over the past years, while the group of research institutes has remained quite similar and the group of other universities has decreased.

Having presented the regionally located co-authors of both German universities, the following figure now demonstrates the supra-regionally distribution of the co-authors of the KIT and Heidelberg:

[72] See appendix for the visualization of both networks with the 76 German universities.

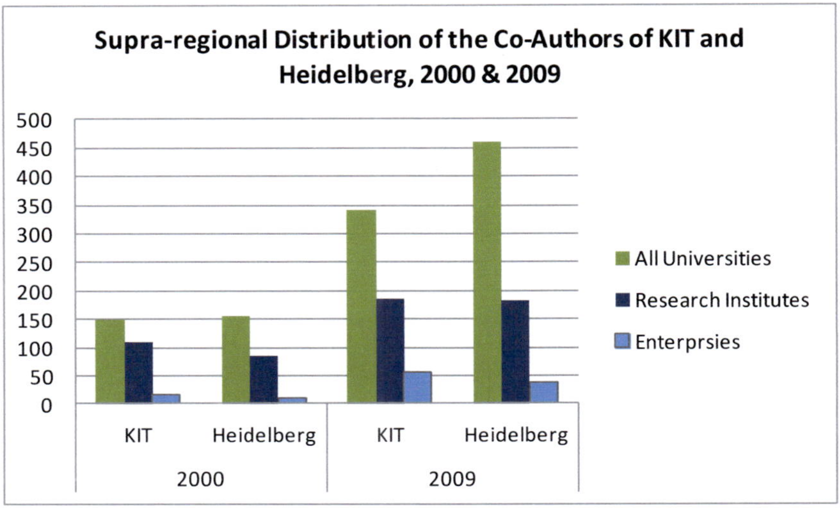

Figure 40: Supra-regional Distribution of the Co-Authors of KIT and Heidelberg, weighted Numbers, 2000 and 2009 (own illustration).

As can be seen from the figure, the KIT and Heidelberg have most often cooperated with partners coming from universities, followed by the group of research institutes and finally the enterprises.

In 2000, 54% of all cooperation partners have come from universities in the case of the KIT and even 62% in the case of Heidelberg. Around one third have been employed at research institutes in the case of Heidelberg, and 40% in the case of the KIT. Finally, only a minor part has come from enterprises, namely 6% at the KIT and 3% in Heidelberg. From 2000 until 2009, the KIT has increased the number of cooperation partners that have come from universities up to 58% as well as the share of enterprises which has already accounted for 10% in 2009. In contrast, the group of research institutes has lost eight percentage points from 2000 until 2009. Heidelberg has increased its cooperation partners that have come from universities and enterprises, while the share of the research institutes has declined over the past ten years.

Referring to the overall distribution, the KIT has especially increased the share of supra-regionally located enterprises during the past ten years, even though in terms of absolute numbers, the KIT still cooperates more likely with regionally located enterprises. In the case of Heidelberg, the share of regionally located research institutes has remained quite similar over the past ten years, while the share of supra-regionally located ones has highly declined from 2000 until 2009.

To sum up, Heidelberg is a bit more engaged in co-authored publications compared to the KIT. However, this finding is not surprising as it confirms the results of the former analysis of all German universities which has shown that the technical universities have been less engaged in co-authored publications compared to the non-technical universities, while the medical universities have more likely cooperated with other partners compared to their counterparts. Further, Heidelberg has been more involved in close network collaborations and has been further more important as intermediary within the knowledge network. It has been also confirmed by the comparison of the KIT and Heidelberg that the technical universities have been more involved in close network collaborations with enterprises, while the medical universities has more likely cooperated research institutes. Finally, it has been discovered that Heidelberg as medical oriented university seems to be more likely engaged with regional cooperation partners compared to the KIT as technical oriented university.

Finally, it is shown how the KIT and Heidelberg has performed regarding their innovation and collaboration activity. For this, the following table firstly illustrates the absolute number of their co-applicants as well as the values of normalized degree and betweenness centrality:

Number of Co-Applicants, Degree and Betweenness Centrality of KIT and Heidelberg, 2003-2004 & 2007-2008				
	2003-2004		2007-2008	
	KIT	Heidelberg	KIT	Heidelberg
Number of Co-Applicants	15	14	20	10
Normalized Degree Centrality	0,019802	0,019802	0,0521739	0,0144928
Betweenness Centrality	0,000306	0,0003278	0,115064	0,0100627

Table 37: Number of Co-Applicants, Degree and Betweenness Centrality of KIT and Heidelberg, 2003-2004 and 2007-2008 (own illustration).

Above table now illustrates that within the first time period, the KIT has possessed 15 co-applicants and Heidelberg has been at the same level with 14 co-applicants. During the past years, while the KIT has increased its number of co-applicants by around 50%, Heidelberg has even experienced a decline by 30%. Regarding the value of normalized degree centrality which can be for example used to compare networks of different size, it is obvious that within the first time period, both universities have still been at the same level, while the performance of

Heidelberg highly decreased over the past years. Hence, in terms of patents, it is the KIT which has been more involved in close network collaborations over the past years and has been more important as knowledge intermediary within the network compared to Heidelberg. However, as the overall activity is still rather small, especially compared to the overall publication activity, it would not be reasonable to show the institutional and spatial distribution of only these two universities. But, the following figure visualizes their overall networks from 1999 until 2008:

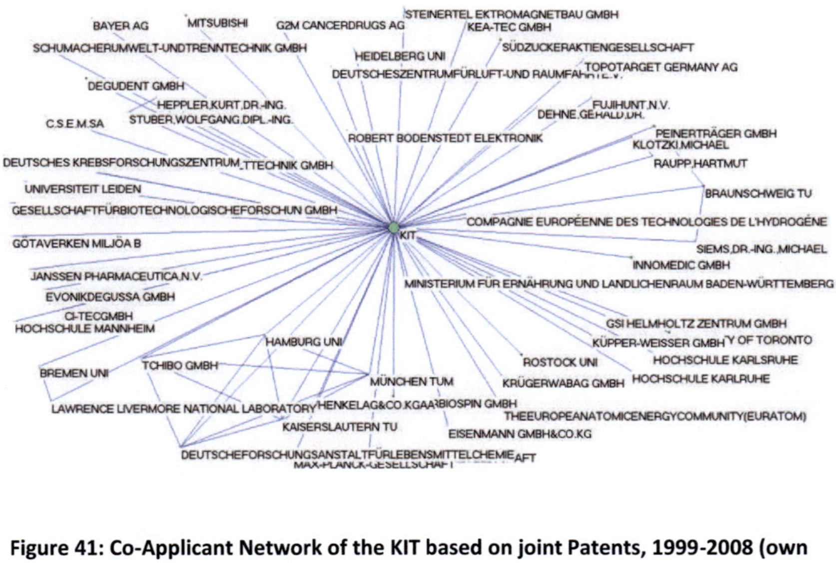

Figure 41: Co-Applicant Network of the KIT based on joint Patents, 1999-2008 (own illustration).

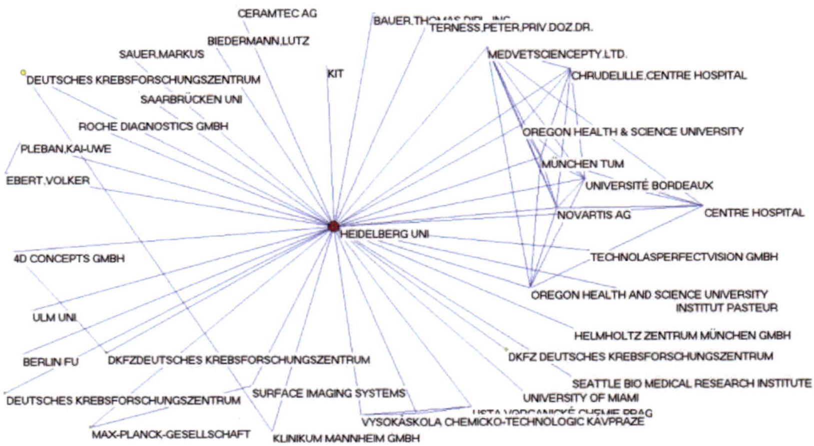

Figure 42: Co-Applicant Network of Heidelberg based on joint Patents, 1999-2008 (own illustration).

As can be seen from the figures, the co-applicant network of the KIT offers a more dynamic development regarding its distinct cooperation partners compared to the one of Heidelberg. Besides, it is obvious that the KIT has rather cooperated with enterprises while Heidelberg has been more engaged with research institutes and universities as already discovered in terms of the publication analysis. Thereby, famous industry partners of the KIT are, amongst other, Bayer, Mitsubishi, Südzucker Mannheim, Fujihunt, Eisenmann, Henkel, Tchibo and Evonik. In contrast, Heidelberg has cooperated with several research institutes as DKFZ Deutsches Krebsforschungszentrum, the Oregon Health and Science University, the Helmholtz Zentrum Munich, the Max-Planck-Gesellschaft and the Seattle Medical Research Institute, amongst other.

Of course, both universities have also cooperated with either renowned research institutions or enterprises respectively.

Overall, it is the KIT which has been more involved in close network collaborations from 1999 until 2008 and has been simultaneously more important as knowledge intermediary within the network compared to Heidelberg. The analysis of the KIT and Heidelberg in terms of patents has finally also confirmed the findings of the broad analysis regarding the whole sample of the German universities.

12. Final Conclusion, Reflection and Policy Recommendations

In the following, the final conclusion firstly presents all relevant results of the empirical analysis, illustrating in how far the four main hypotheses could have been confirmed or had to be rejected. Afterwards, a comprehensive reflection of the empirical results is shown accompanied by several policy recommendations. In this context, it is aimed to highlight potentials of the German academic landscape as well as possible constraints in order to be prepared for new challenges in a world where competition has become increasingly knowledge-based. In doing so, it is aimed to ensure that the German knowledge-based economy can further develop, providing sustainable economic growth rates and remaining competitive in our ever more globalised world.

12.1. Final Conclusion

In order to present a comprehensive and well structured final conclusion of this PhD thesis, all relevant results of the four main hypotheses are illustrated separately. Hence, the following subsections refer to all important findings with regard to the knowledge generation, innovation and collaboration activities of the German universities.

Knowledge Generation, Innovation and Collaboration

To be able to show a first broad overview of the empirical results of this first main part, the following table shows the first hypothesis and its outcome:

Summary of the emprical Results - Part 1		
	Hypothesis	**Outcome**
Knowledge Generation, Innovation and Collaboration	*H1: Scientific publications and patent applications have highly increased over time and collaborations for knowledge and innovation have become much more important.*	***confirmed*** *in terms of publications*
		confirmed *in terms of patents*

Table 38: Summary of the empirical Results (own illustration).

Starting with the publication activity of the German universities, it is to be stated that they have shown high rates of published papers in renowned journals over the past ten years. In 2000, they have already been involved in around 44,000 publications, but could increase this number by 70 % in 2009. Besides, while they have still published more often on their own in 2000, this development has absolutely strongly changed during the last ten years. In 2009, they have been overall engaged in almost 80,000 publications at all, but only about 28,000 have come from single-authorship. Thus, publication and collaboration activity continuously rose over the time period from 2000 until 2009, while single-authorship has increased by only 18% compared to 125%

regarding co-authorship. Thus, hypothesis 1 is confirmed in terms of publications.

Besides, this PhD thesis could also confirm that the German universities have seen a huge increase regarding their number of filed patents. While they have filed around 281 patents from 1999 until 2000, they could already triple their number of patent applications within the time period 2007 until 2008. In all, it can be concluded that the behaviour of the German universities has strongly changed over the past ten years, as they operate much more often as applicants themselves, hence, being less dependent on other institutional actors anymore. Overall, it can be stated that not only the patenting activity of the German universities in terms of filed patents has highly increased over the past ten years, but the number of co-applicants, too. Over the past ten years, the German universities have seen an increase of around 150% regarding the number of co-applicants. Hence, hypothesis 1 is also confirmed in terms of patents.

From merely Knowledge Producers towards Knowledge Mediators

The following part refers to the increasing meaning of the German universities as central nodes for knowledge and innovation transfer. Table 39 summarizes the empirical results of this part:

Summary of the emprical Results - Part 2		
	Hypothesis	**Outcome**
From merely Knowledge Producers towards Knowledge Mediators	*H2: The role of the German universities has changed from merely knowledge producers towards knowledge mediators, which leads to an increasing importance of universities as a central node for knowledge and innovation transfer.*	***largely confirmed*** *in terms of publications*
		confirmed *in terms of patents*

Table 39: Summary of the empirical Results (own illustration).

Coming to hypothesis 2, it has to be mentioned that referring to the institutional distribution of the German university co-authors, network collaborations with universities are still most important, but university-industry linkages have had a more dynamic development. Further, the value of normalized degree centrality has, amongst other, shown that the German universities could have increased their distinct cooperation partners over the past ten years, as the value has risen by around 20%. Thereby, the top three German universities in 2009 are Heidelberg (0.091701), the Technical University of Munich (0.0865566) and the LMU Munich (0.796075). But, regarding the mean value of betweenness centrality, it has been eye-catching that it has not increased over the past ten years, but decreased from around 0.026 to 0.024. Thus, the German university networks have indeed become larger at the expense of a decreasing mean value of betweenness centrality which probably means that the overall network itself has become less dense. Overall, hypothesis 2 is largely confirmed in terms of publications.

Regarding the institutional distribution of the cooperation partners of the German universities in terms of joint patent applications, it is obvious that the German universities have had only 209 co-applicants within the first time period but could raise this number up to 468 within the time period from 2007 until 2008. Further, they have most often cooperated with enterprises, but the highest increase of co-applicants can be observed within the group of research institutes (plus 540%), even though the absolute number of those partnerships has always been much lower compared to the one of the enterprises. In all, a strongly growing importance of the German universities as co-applicants in innovation networks can be observed, especially with regard to close network collaborations with enterprises. Further, as it applies for the publication data, the German universities have also highly increased their distinct co-applicants over the past ten years, as the value has increased by around 120%. Of course, the dynamics regarding the development of the number of distinct co-applicants is much higher compared to the one of the co-authors as in terms of patents, they have possessed a rather low value within the first time period but could greatly advance themselves. Further, the top three German universities within the last time period are Erlangen-Nürnberg (0.0608496), Würzburg (0.0608696) and the KIT (0.0521739). Other than the mean value of betweenness centrality based on publications, the German universities could also highly increase their mean value of betweenness centrality regarding their innovation networks. Thus, hypothesis 2 is fully confirmed in terms of patents.

In all, it is obvious that the German universities have shown different behavioural patterns regarding their publication and patenting activities, as, for example, the top three German universities regarding the highest value of normalized degree centrality differ in this regard. Thus, up to now, it has already been discovered that there are first differences regarding the behavioural patterns of the German universities.

Last, it has also been shown that third-party funds have had a highly significant effect on the collaboration activity of the German universities with enterprises regarding joint papers. Reasons for the significance of third party funds can be constituted in the fact that most of those funds have come from the private sector which, in turn, has led to more collaborations and co-authored publications with enterprises. Besides, third-party funds have had also a significant effect on the patenting activity of the German universities. This finding is not surprising either, as linkages to enterprises have made up the highest share of collaborations. In all, the OLS regression model has underpinned the results that university-industry interactions are not only prevalent but also gaining much more importance so that industry partners are highly valuable in the system of knowledge generation and innovation for the German universities.

Proximity Patterns in Times of Globalization

The concluding remarks regarding proximity patterns in times of globalisation also starts with an overview of the empirical result in tabular form:

Summary of the emprical Results - Part 3		
	Hypothesis	**Outcome**
Proximity Patterns in Times of Globalisation	*H3: Spatial Proximity has lost in importance regarding close network collaborations concerning knowledge spillovers between the German universities and other institutional cooperation partners.*	***Partially confirmed*** *in terms of publications*

Table 40: Summary of the empirical Results (own illustration).

Factors as the growth of multinationals, global markets and the fast diffusion of the ICT may have led to the assumption that proximity patterns matter less nowadays. There are many new opportunities for enterprises and institutions which make it possible to nearly completely neglect spatial proximity. However, the results of this PhD thesis have given further insight into the question of proximity patterns in an ever more globalised world.

Considering all co-authors within the 1,000 km radius, it could have been discovered that especially those co-authors who have been located within a radius of 100 km have been most important for the German universities as potential cooperation partners. Further, scaling down the size of the distance corridor to 25 km, it could have been even emphasized that especially locality still plays a major role for the German universities. While in 2009, around 2,500 co-authors have been located within the first (0 km - >25 km) distance corridor, the second one (25 km - >50 km) has only possessed around 500 co-authors. Overall, the values of Spearman's rank correlation coefficient have shown a quite strong and negative effect. In 2000, the value has been -0.80 and in 2009 even -0.85 regarding the spatial distribution of the German university co-authors between 0 km and 1,000 km. This means that the number of co-authors declines with the growth of distance. Thus, up to now, above hypothesis needs to be rejected.

But, it seems likely that the value of Spearman's rank correlation coefficient has been just as high because of the huge number of co-authors within the first distance corridor (0 km - <25 km). Moreover, it has been shown that those co-authors who have been located anywhere between 25 km and <475 km have been more or less equally distributed within their particular distance corridors, while spatial proximity did again matter from about 475 km onwards. Thus, in case that the co-authors of the first distance corridor have not been considered anymore as well as those that have been anywhere located >474 km, it could have been shown that the German universities did not further consider distance for the choice of their cooperation partners. Hence, above hypothesis is to be partially confirmed.

To briefly sum up above findings, it has to be said that while locality still seems to highly matter regarding the choice of the cooperation partners of the German universities, regional distance between 25 km and <475 km does not seem to play a role, but from 475 km onwards the friction of distance have started weight again. Hence, above hypothesis is finally to be partially confirmed.[73]

Last, considering all co-authors of the German universities, either being regional (0 km – 468 km) or supra-regional (>468 km) located, it has been discovered that the spatial distribution of the German university co-authors is more or less equally distributed.[74] Further, regarding the spatial distribution of the different institutional cooperation partners of the German universities, it has been shown that especially research and industry partners have become more regionally distributed, while the share of universities being regionally or supra-regionally distributed has remained quite similar from 2000 until 2009, even though the German universities have slightly increased their cooperations with supra-regionally located universities. However, in all it can be said that regional cooperations have slightly gained in importance, while supra-regional co-authors have lost a bit in importance over the past ten years.

[73] See chapter six for the determination of the distance classes.
[74] See chapter six for the determination of the distance classes.

<u>Analysis of the three different groups of German universities</u>

After having concluded how the German universities as the whole group did behave regarding their knowledge, innovation and collaboration activities with special consideration of the spatial dimension, this final part refers to the behavioural patterns of the three different types of German universities. Hence, the following table firstly illustrates the outcome of all relevant hypotheses in this regard:

Summary of the emprical Results - Part 4				
	Main Hypothesis 4: Cooperation patterns differ in case of considering different groups of German universities.	**Outcome**		
		Technical and non-technical	**Medical and non-medical**	**Elite and non-elite**
Analysis of the three different Groups of German Universities	*H4a: The technical, medical [and elite] universities are more engaged in close network collaborations than their counterparts due to high cost of research and pooling of resources.*	***rejected*** *in terms of publications*	***partially confirmed*** *in terms of publications*	***no significant results*** *in terms of publications*
		no significant results *in terms of patents*	***confirmed*** *in terms of patents*	***confirmed*** *in terms of patents*
	H4b: The technical [and elite] universities are more likely to cooperate with industrial partners due to a higher degree in applied research compared to their counterparts. In contrast, the medical universities do cooperate more often with knowledge-intensive institutions as universities and research institutes due to a higher degree in basic research-intensive bias.	***confirmed*** *in terms of publications*	***confirmed*** *in terms of publications*	***no significant results*** *in terms of publications*
		largely confirmed *in terms of patents*	***largely confirmed*** *in terms of patents*	***largely confirmed*** *in terms of patents*
	H4c: The technical and elite universities are rather engaged in collaborations with supra-regional partners compared to the non-technical and non-elite universities. The medical universities are more likely to cooperate with regional partners than the non-medical universities.	***confirmed*** *in terms of publications*	***confirmed*** *in terms of publications*	***confirmed*** *in terms of publications*

Table 41: Summary of the empirical Results (own illustration).

Up till now, there is no doubt that the overall publication, patenting and collaboration activity of all German universities has highly increased over the past ten years. However, the empirical results of the last main hypothesis have discovered significant differences between the three different groups of German universities as above table already indicates.

Before referring to hypothesis 4a in terms of publications, a non parametric median test has previously been conducted which has discovered that the medical as well as the elite universities have generally published more often compared to their counterparts. This does not apply for the technical universities as they have a similar median as the non-technical universities. Coming to their cooperation activity, above table shows that in terms of publications the non-technical universities have more often cooperated than the technical universities, even though they have not offered any differences regarding their publication activity. Further, in 2000, the non-medical universities have been more likely engaged in co-authored publications, while in 2009, it is the group of medical universities that has cooperated more often with other partners. Hence, the behavioural patterns in this regard have changed in favor of the medical universities within the last time period. This changing development could have been largely explained by the value of normalized degree centrality, as it has highly increased for the medical universities over the past ten years, while it has even declined for the non-medical universities. Last, no significant results have been found for the group of the elite and non-elite universities in this regard, even though the elite universities have indeed published more often compared to the non-elite universities. Regarding the institutional distribution of the German university co-authors, it has been demonstrated by hypothesis 4b that the technical universities have cooperated more often with enterprises than the non-technical universities. Further, the non-medical universities have had more linkages to enterprises over the past ten years compared to the medical universities. Finally, concerning the group of elite and non-elite universities, no significant differences could have been found in this regard again.

Coming to the innovation and collaboration activity of the three different groups of German universities in terms of patents, a non parametric median test regarding the value of betweenness centrality has been conducted in order to explore hypothesis 4a. Thereby, it has been discovered that the medical and elite universities have been more likely engaged in close network cooperations compared to their counterparts. For the group of technical and non-technical universities the median test has not brought up a significant result. Further, coming to the institutional distribution of their cooperation partners, it has firstly been shown that the absolute number of enterprises as well as its increase is very strong in each group. In this context, it has been especially striking that the medical universities have experienced the largest increase of private enterprises as institutional partners which amounts to 1,000%. In all, it is the enterprises which seem to require more academic knowledge as the rising number of partnerships expresses. However, the empirical results have anyway confirmed hypothesis 4b, as the elite and technical universities have more likely cooperated with enterprises than their counterparts, and the medical universities have cooperated more often with research institutes and universities compared to the non-medical universities.[75]

Further, hypothesis 4c assumes that there are significant differences regarding proximity patterns when the three different groups of German universities are examined and compared with each other in terms of their publication activity. Above table well documents that hypothesis 4c could be entirely confirmed. Thus, it is the elite and the technical universities that have more likely cooperated with supra-regional co-authors compared to their counterparts. Besides, the medical universities have been more likely to cooperate with regionally located partners compared to the non-medical universities. Hence, it is still prevalent that due to the important role of trust in medical knowledge collaborations, proximity patterns still highly matter.

Due to the previous results, it has been further assumed that the technical and elite universities have been rather engaged with supra-regionally located enterprises compared to their counterparts, while the

---

[75] The empirical results have been only significant for the first time period in case of the medical and non-medical and elite and non-elite universities. The technical and non-technical universities have had still slight significant differences within the last time period.

medical universities have more often cooperated with regionally located research institutes and universities compared to the non-medical universities. In this context, it is further surprising that it has been the non-technical universities that have rather cooperated with supra-regionally located enterprises and not the technical ones. Thus, above made assumption has to be rejected as the technical universities have been indeed more engaged with enterprises and with supra-regionally located cooperation partners in general, but not with supra-regionally located enterprises but with supra-regionally research institutes and universities. Besides, it has been the medical universities that have more likely cooperated with regionally located research institutes and universities compared to their counterparts and the elite universities have been more engaged with supra-regionally located enterprises compared to the non-elite universities as assumed above.

Last, it has been looked at the spatial distribution of the German university co-authors based on their country codes. In this context, it has been basically proved whether the medical, technical and elite universities have been more likely to cooperate with partners coming from North America and from EU14 than from emerging countries as BRIC. Thereby, it has been discovered that the medical universities have most likely cooperated with partners coming from North America, while partners from EU14 have occupied second place. It has been further conspicuous that the medical universities have more likely either cooperated with North America or with EU14 than with the emerging countries as BRIC compared to their counterparts. Thus, the medical universities have not changed their cooperation manner in favour of the emerging countries, but still highly trust in the well-known 'Western knowledge'. Also in case of JANZ, the medical universities have more likely cooperated with North American partners. In contrast, the technical universities have indeed more often cooperated with partners coming from EU14 than from North America compared to the non-technical universities. But in case of potential collaborations with partners either coming from BRIC or from North America and EU14, the technical universities have decided in both cases in favor of BRIC. Besides, they have continuously been more likely engaged in close network collaborations with JANZ than with North America and EU14. Thus, the technical universities highly trust in knowledge-intensive interactions with the emerging countries as well as with JANZ which are furthest away from Germany. In case of the elite and non-elite universities, there are only a few significant results. In all, they have also been more engaged in close network collaborations with North America and the EU14 than with the emerging countries as BRIC compared to the non-elite universities.

12.2. Reflection and Policy Recommendations

To come back to the statement of Francis Bacon from the introduction of this PhD thesis, it is beyond question that the German universities highly contribute to knowledge generation, innovation and are highly involved in close network collaborations so that the old statement gains even more in importance. In an ever more globalised world, it is not an easy task to remain competitive and to retain sustainable economic growth rates. Thus, it is of high interest to invest in human capital as human capital remains economic power.

The empirical results of the first part regarding the knowledge generation, innovation and collaboration potential of the German universities have especially shown that in case of joint publications, university-industry interactions have observed a more dynamic development compared to the still important university-university linkages. But in absolute numbers, it is of course the universities themselves who are more likely to cooperate with each other. Thus, policy measures should further aim to stimulate cooperations especially between universities and enterprises. Thereby, it is of high interest that both sides, industry and university, benefit from the development of sustainable structures from policy makers. Hence, policy programs as the Hightech Strategy initiated by the BMBF which, amongst other, support knowledge-intensive cooperations between industry and the research community, have already been the right policy choice but should be intensively pursued and further extended.

Besides, it is also beyond question that an increasing integration of university research and non-university research is also of high interest and remains trend-setting. At the moment, collaboration activities between the German universities and research institutes have not grown as fast as interactions among universities. While collaborations with research institutes have been more frequently occurred in 2000 compared to the famous university-university interactions, today, this development has changed in favor of the universities. Thus, when the German universities aim to get on a level with, for example, their US competitors, public policy measures should concentrate on stimulating those interactions, too. The KIT which was founded by a merger of Forschungszentrum Karlsruhe and Universität Karlsruhe or the foundation of the RWTH Campus GmbH[76] which, amongst other, incorporates university and non-univeristy research as well as industry research are good examples how to shape the German knowledge-based future in order to be able to compete with famous institutions such as the MIT.

Moreover, there is no doubt that the patenting activity of the German universities has increased over the past ten years, but it is still far away from industry patenting as well as from industry cooperation activity in terms of joint patents. Thus, regarding the innovative potential of the German universities regarding the number of filed patents and co-applicants, policy measures need to be created that explicitly affect these concerns. Against this background, it could be beneficial to foster

[76] A German 'Gesellschaft mit beschränkter Haftung (GmbH)' is synonymous with the English Limited (Ltd). For further information on this topic, see http://www.rwth-aachen.de/cms/root/Wirtschaft/~ekt/Campusprojekt// 15.04.2013.

and to improve transfer processes by establishing transfer models in order to increase the level of innovation among universities, enterprises and research institutes. In this context, it is further evident that third-party funds have increased the overall patenting activity of the German universities. Bearing this in mind, the logical conclusion is to provide policy measures that further stimulate collaborations between the broader research community and industry, in order to ensure valuable joint innovations. Here, it could be possible that missing frame conditions regarding property rights constitute an important issue as they are probably debilitating for joint patents. It is surely difficult for universities, research institutes and enterprises to agree on manifold questions concerning intellectual property rights. Therefore, a proper framework should be developed in this regard in order to avoid that inventions remain secretly, as an economy is only able to benefit from new knowledge if it is aware of it. Here, the aforementioned transfer models could be productive, too, amongst other.

In all, the SNA has already discovered that the German universities behave differently regarding their publication and patenting activity. As already discussed in the previous subchapter, it is the KIT, the University of Erlangen and the University of Würzburg that have had most distinct co-applicants, while the Technical University of Munich, the LMU Munich and the University of Heidelberg have been mostly engaged in close network collaborations in terms of joint publications. Thus, it seems reasonable that some universities are more traditionally oriented than others who have rather turned to more entrepreneurial units.[77] However, it is natural to explore why a given university is more engaged in either joint patenting or joint publications to be further able to provide the right policy choice. In this context, the separate analysis of the KIT and Heidelberg, as a technical compared to a medical university, has shown that the KIT has been more engaged in joint patents, while Heidelberg has been more likely to publish in cooperation. Hence, further studies should explore this phenomenon in order to provide each university with the right policy choice. Besides, it has been discovered that both in terms of publications and patents, the technical universities have been more likely to cooperate with industrial partners, while the medical universities have cooperated more often with knowledge-intensive institutions compared to their particular counterparts. Thus, it might be further worth to examine why they behave accordingly, aiming to simultaneously develop specific public policy measures that support newer forms of cooperations as public-private-partnerships (PPP) to join industry partners as well as the research community likewise. It is beyond question that diversification is especially worth regarding the emergence of new knowledge, technology and finally innovations.

This PhD thesis has further demonstrated that proximity patterns still matter in an ever more globalised world as especially locality still plays a

[77] A traditional university can of course also be very active regarding joint patenting as an entrepreneurial university is also highly engaged in joint publications.

crucial role regarding the choice of the cooperation partners of the German universities. Against this background, public policy measures should of course further aim to support local cooperations, as the integration of various organizations within a particular region can bring about economic strength and can also attract the setting up of other foreign organizations. Thus, policy measures that strengthen a particular region and help to build up trust in this region may simultaneously stimulate national and international partnerships. Of course, there is no doubt that it is compulsive to foster knowledge-intensive cooperations within Germany or within a particular region of Germany; nevertheless, knowledge and experience from different countries or from different cultural regions may further stimulate the emergence of high-quality innovations that can be valuable for everyone. As especially linkages to supra-regionally-located enterprises have lost in importance over the past ten years, policy measures should of course not only foster domestic partnerships, but also consider global players and foreign markets in order to benefit from national as well as from international knowledge.

It has been further discovered that the elite and the technical universities have more likely cooperated with supra-regional co-authors compared to their counterparts, and the medical universities have been more likely to cooperate with regionally located partners compared to the non-medical universities. These findings could have been also confirmed by the separate analysis of the KIT and Heidelberg. Hence, it is still prevalent that due to the important role of trust in medical knowledge collaborations, proximity patterns still highly matter in this regard. Further, in case the medical universities have cooperated with partners coming from abroad, they mainly trust in the well-known Western knowledge as they have been most likely to cooperate with partners coming from North America than from BRIC. Also in case of JANZ, the medical universities have more likely cooperated with North American partners. It might be worth offering policy measures that aim to deepen trust, even though the cooperation partner is far away or comes from an emerging country. There are certainly hidden potentials that can be further used to strengthen competitiveness and to bring up new knowledge and technologies. In this context, exploring whether the medical universities have been more likely to cooperate with partners coming from North America or from EU14, it has been shown that they have decided in favour of North America compared to their counterparts. Hence, it should be worked on better framework conditions in terms of inventive programmes at the European level, too, in order to strengthen Europe. Regarding the technical and non-technical universities, it is somewhat the other way round, as they have cooperated more often with BRIC than with EU14 or North America. Thus, it is generally beneficial to develop and provide comprehensive public policy measures that also affect at the European level and can be further followed within the European research frame programme Horizon 2020[78].

[78] For further information on this issue see http://ec.europa.eu/research/horizon2020/index_en.cfm, 27.04.2013.

In conclusion, it has been shown by this PhD thesis that the German universities are not only powerful with regard to their knowledge generation and innovation function but they are also highly involved in knowledge-intensive network interactions. Thus, as knowledge remains economic power, the German universities strongly contribute to the local, regional and national development of the German knowledge-based economy.

13. References

Abramson, H. N., Encarnacao, J., Reid, P. P., & Schmoch, U. (1997). *Technology Transfer Systems in the United States and Germany.* Washington: National Academy Press.

Acs, Z., Anselin, L., & Varga, A. (1997). Local geographic spillovers between university research and high technology innovations. *Journal of Urban Economics, Vol. 42, Is. 3* , pp. 422–448.

Adams, J. (2002). Comparative localization of academic and industrial spillovers. *Journal of Economic Geography, Vol. 2* , pp. 253-278.

Aldrich, H. E., & Zimmer, C. (1986). Entrepreneurship Through Social Networks. *University of Illinois at Urbana-Champaign's Academy for Entrepreneurial Leadership Historical Research Reference in Entrepreneurship* , pp. 1-32.

Anselin, L., Acs, J., & Varga, A. (2002). Patents and innovation counts as measures of regional production of new knowledge. *Research Policy Vol. 31* , pp. 1069-1085.

Archinugi, D., & Coco, A. (2004). International partnerships for knowledge in business and academia: A comparison between Europe and the USA. *Technovation, Vol. 24* , pp. 517-528.

Arundel, A., & Geuna, A. (2004). Proximity and the use of public science by innovative European firms. *Economics of Innovation and New Technologies Vol. 13, No. 3* , pp. 559-580.

Asheim, B., & Isaksen, A. (1997). Localisation, Agglomeration and Innovation: Towards regional Innovation Systems in Norway? European Planning Studies, 5, 3: 299-330. *European Planning Studies, Vol. 5, No. 3* , pp. 299-330.

Audretsch, D. (1998). AGGLOMERATION AND THE LOCATION OF INNOVATIVE ACTIVITY. *OXFORD REVIEW OF ECONOMIC POLICY, VOL. 14, NO. 2* , pp. 18-29.

Bacon, F. (1597). *Meditationes Sacrae.* Meditationes Sacrae.

Becker, G. S. (1994). *Human Capital: A Theoretical and Empirical Analysis with Special Reference to Education.* Chicago: The University Chicago Press, 3rd Edition.

Becker, W. (2003). Evaluation of the Role of Universities. *Working Paper 241, University of Augsburg* , pp. 1-26.

Bellgardt, E. (2004). *Statistik mit SPSS.* 2. überarbeitete Auflage, Vahlen.

Berman, E. (1990). The economic impact of industry-funded university R&D. *Research Policy, Vol. 19* , pp. 349–355.

Bertram, B. (2011). Innovationsprozesse wissensbasierter Technologien - Beispiel der PEM-Brennstoffzelle. Karlsruhe: KIT Scientific Publishing.

Blackler, F. (1995). Knowledge, knowledge work and organisations: an overview and interpretation. *Organization Studies, Vol. 16* , pp. 1021-1046.

BMBF. (2004). *Forschungslandkarte Fachhochschulen - Potentialstudie.* Bonn und Berlin.

BMBF. (2012). *Wissenschaft, Hochschule, Exzellenzinitiative*. Retrieved from http://www.bmbf.de/de/1321.php, 06/09/2012

Borch, O. J., & Arthur, M. B. (1995). Strategic Networks among Small Firms: Implications for Strategy Research Methodology. *Journal of Management Studies Vol. 32, No. 4* , pp. 420-441.

Borchert, J., Philipp, G., & Hagenhoff, S. (2004). Innovationsnetzwerke als Quelle von Wettbewerbsvorteilen. *Working Paper No. 11, M. Schumann (Ed.)* .

Bosch, K. (1996). *Großes Lehrbuch der Statistik.* München: Oldenbourg Verlag GmbH.

Boschma, R. (2005). Proximity and Innovation: A Critical Assessment. *Regional Studies, Vol. 39* , pp. 61-74.

Breschi, S., & Lissoni, F. (2001). Localised knowledge spillovers vs. innovative millieux: knowledge "tacitness" reconsidered. *Regional Science, Vol. 80* , 255-273.

Breschi, S., & Lissoni, F. (2003). Mobility and Social Networks: Localised Knowledge Spillover Revisited. *CESPRI, Working Paper No. 142* , pp. 1-29.

Burnham, J. F. (2006). Scopus database: a review. *Biomedical Digital Libraries, Resource Review* , pp. 1-8.

Camagni, R. (2001). The economic role and spatial contradictions of global city-regions: the functional, cognitive and evolutionary context. *Scott A. (2001)* , pp. 96-118.

Cantner, U., & Graf, H. (2006). The network of innovators in Jena: An application of social network analysis. *Research Policy, Vol. 35, No. 4* , pp. 463-480.

Carpenter, M., & Narin, F. (1983). Validation Study: Patents Citations as Indicators of Science and foreign Dependence. *Wold Patent Information, Vol. 5, Is. 3* , pp. 180-185.

Chandy, R., Hopstaken, B., Narasimhan, O., & Prabhu, J. (2006). From Invention to Innovation: Conversion Ability in Product Development. *Journal of Marketing Research, Vol. 43* , pp. 494–508.

Christ, J. (2007). *Varieties of Systems of Innovation: A Survey of their Evolution in Growth Theory and Economic Geography.* Hohenheim: Schriftenreihe des Promotionsschwerpunkts Globalisierung und Beschäftigung.

Cohen, W. M., & Levinthal, D. A. (1990). Absorptive Capacity: A New Perspective on Learning and Innovation. *Administrative Science Quarterly, Vol. 35, No. 1* , pp. 128-152.

Cohen, W. M., Nelson, R. R., & Walsh, J. P. (2002). Protecting Their Intellectual Assets: Appropriability Conditions and Why U.S. Manufacturing Firms Patent (or Not). *NBER Working Paper No. 7552* , pp. 1-31.

Cooke, P. (2001). Regional Innovation Systems, Clusters, and the Knowledge Economy. *Industrial and Corporate Change, Vol. 10, No. 4* , pp. 945-974.

Cooke, P., Uranga, M., & Etxebarria, G. (1997). Regional Innovation Systems, Institutional and Organisastional Dimensions. *Research Policy, Vol. 26, IS 4-5* , pp. 475-491.

Coombs, R., Narandren, P., & Richards, A. (1996). A literature-based innovation output indicator. *Research Policy, Vol. 25, No.3* , pp. 403-413.

Cowan, R., David, A., & Foray, D. (2000). The Explicit Economics of Knowledge Codification and Tacitness. *Industrial and Corporate Change, Vol. 9, No. 2* , pp. 211-253.

DESTATIS. (2010). *Bildung und Kultur - Monetäre hochschulstatistische Kennzahlen.* Wiesbaden: Statistisches Bundesamt, Fachserie 11 Reihe 4.3.2.

DESTATIS. (2011). *Statistisches Bundesamt*. Retrieved from Zahlen und Fakten, Hochschulen insgesamt: https://www.destatis.de/DE/ZahlenFakten/GesellschaftStaat/BildungForschungKultur/Hochschulen/Tabellen/HochschulenHochschularten.html

DESTATIS. (2012). *Statistisches Bundesamt*. Retrieved from https://www.destatis.de/DE/Startseite.html

Oxford Dictionaries. (2012). Bibliography. http://oxforddictionaries.com/definition/english/bibliography.

Edquist, C. (2001). *Innovation Policy. A Systematic Approach.* Oxford: University Press.

Edquist, C. (2005). Systems of Innovation: Perspectives and Challenges. *Fagerberg, Jan, Mowery, David C. and Nelson, Richard R. (eds.), The Oxford Handbook of Innovation, Oxford University Press* , pp. 181-208.

Edquist, C. (1997). *Systems of Innovation: Technologies, Institutions and Organizations.* London: Pinter.

Edquist, C. (2001). The System of Innovation Approach and Innovation Policy: An accountof the state of the art DRUID Conference, Aalborg, June 12-15, 2001. *DRUID Conference, Aalborg* .

EFI-Gutachten. (2012). *Gutachten zur Forschung, Innovation und technologischer Leistungsfähigkeit, Expertenkommission Forschung und Innovation.* Berlin: http://www.e-fi.de/fileadmin/Gutachten/EFI_Gutachten_2012_deutsch.pdf.

Ejermo, O. (2009). Regional Innovation Measured By Patent Data - Does Quality Matter? *Industry and Innovation, Vol. 16, No. 2* , pp. 141-165.

Etkowitz, H., & Leydesdorff, L. (2000). The dynamics of innovation: from National Systems and 'Mode 2' to a Triple Helix of university-industry government relations. *Research Policy* , pp. 109-123.

Etzkowitz, H. (1989). Entrepreneurial Science in the Academy: A Case of the Transformation of Norms. *Social Problems, Vol. 36, No. 1* , pp. 14-29.

Etzkowitz, H. (1998). The Norms of Entrepreneurial Science: Cognitive Effects of the New University-Industry Linkages. *Research Policy, Vol. 27* , pp. 823-834.

Falagras, M. E., Pitsouni, E. I., Malietzis, G. A., & Pappas, G. (2008). Comparison of PubMed, Scopus, Web of Science, and Google Scholar: strength and weaknesses. *The FASEB Journal* , pp. 338-342.

Fischer, M. M. (2006). The New Economy and Networking. In M. Fischer, *Innovation, Networks, and Knowledge Spillovers, Selected Essays* (pp. 95-115). Berlin Heidelberg: Springer.

Florida, R., Gates, G., Knudsen, B., & Stolarick, K. (2006). The University and the Creative Economy. Working Paper.

Freeman, C. (1987). *Technology Policy and Economic Performance: Lessons from Japan.* London: Frances Pinter.

Freeman, C., & Soete, L. (2009). Developing science, technology and innovation indicaindicators: What we can learn from the past. *Research Policy, Vol. 38* , pp. 583-589.

Frietsch, R., & Jung, T. (2008). *Transnational Patents – Structures, Trends and Recent Developments.* www.e-fi.de: Studie zum deutschen Innovationssystem Nr. XX-2009, Expertenkommission für Forschung und Innovation.

Frietsch, R., Köhler, F., & Blind, K. (2008). *Weltmarktpatente – Strukturen und deren Veränderungen.* www.e-fi.de: Studie zum deutschen Innovationssystem Nr. 7-2008, Expertenkommission für Forschung und Innovation.

Gellert, W., Gottwald, S., Hellwich, M., Kästner, H., & Küstner, H. (1989). *The VNR Concise Encyclopedia of Mathematics.* New York: Van Nostrand Reinhold.

Gelsing, L. (1992). *Innovation and development of industrial networks, in: B. Lundvall (Ed.), Nationale Systems of Innovation: Towards a Theory of Innovation and Interactive Learning.* London: Pinter Publisher.

Glückler, J. (2007). Economic Geography and the Evolution of Networks. *Journal of Economic Geography, Vol. 7, IS. 5* , pp. 619-634.

Godin, B. (2007). National Innovation System: The System Approach in Historical Perspective. *Project on the History and Sociology of STI Statistics: Working Paper No. 36* .

Godin, B., & Gingras, Y. (2000). What is Scientific Culture and How to Measure it: A Multidimensional Model. *Public Understanding of Science, Vol. 9, No. 1* , pp. 43-58.

Griliches, Z. (1990). Patent Statistics as Economic Indicators: A Survey. *Journal of Economic Literature, Vol. 28, No. 4* , pp. 1661-1707.

Griliches, Z. (1984). *R&D, Patents, and Productivity.* University of Chicago Press.

Grodal, S. (2004). Industrial dynamics, innovation and development. *Working Paper presented at the Druid Summer Conference 2004* , pp. 1-28.

Grossman, G., & Helpman, E. (1991). *Innovation and Growth in the Global Economy.* Cambridge: Cambridge: MIT Press.

Grupp, H. (1998). *Messung und Erklärung des technischen Wandels.* Berlin Heidelberg: Springer.

Hagedoorn, J. (1993). Understanding the rationale of strategic technology partnering: inter-organizational modes of cooperation andsectoral differences. *Strategic Management Journal, Vol. 14* , pp. 371-380.

Hamermesh, D. S., & Oster, S. M. (2002). Tools or Toys? The Impact of High Technology on Scholarly Productivity. *Economic Inquiry, Vol. 40, No. 4* , pp. 539-555.

Hancock, J. T., & Dunham, P. J. (2001). Impression Formation in Computer-Mediated Communication Revisited: An Analysis of Impressions. *Communication Research, Vol. 28* , 325-347.

Hochschulrahmengesetz. (2005). *BMBF.* Retrieved from http://www.bmbf.de/pub/HRG_20050126.pdf

Hoogendoorn, G. (2008). Scopus: The Continuing Development of an Abstract and Citation Database. *The Serials Librarian, Vol. 55, Is. 1-2* , pp. 227-234.

Howells, J. (2002). Tacit Knowledge, Innovation and Economic Geography. *Sage, Urban Studies Journal Foundation, Vol. 39, No. 5-6* , pp. 871-884.

Hunt, S. D., & Morgan, R. M. (2000). Global Marketing. *Marketing Management, Vol. 3, No. 1* , pp. 18-28.

Jaffe, A. B. (1989). Real affects of academic research . *The American Economic Review, Vol. 79, No. 5* , pp. 957-970.

Jaffe, A. B., Trajtenberg, M., & Henderson, R. (1993). Geographic localization of knowledge spillovers as evidenced by patent citations. *Quarterly Journal of Economics, Vol. 434* , pp. 578-598.

Johnson, D. K., & Lybecker, K. M. (2012). Does Distance Matter Less Now? The Changing Role of Geography in Biotechnology Innovation. *Springer Rev Ind Organ, Vol. 40* , pp. 21-35.

Karlsson, C., & Zhang, W.-B. (2001). The role of universities in regional development - Endogenous human capital and growth in a two-region model. *The Annals of Regional Science, Vol. 35, No. 2* , pp. 179-197.

Katila, R., & Ahuia, G. (2002). Something old, somethin new: A longitudinal Study od Search Behavior and new Product Introduction. *Academy of Management Journal, Vol. 45, No. 6* , pp. 1183-1194.

Katz, J. S., & Hicks, D. (1997). How much is a collaboration worth? A calibrated bibliometric model. *Scientometrics, Vol. 40, No. 3* , 541–554.

Kim, J. L., & Marschke, G. (2005). The Influence of University Research on Industrial Innovation. *Working Paper presented on NBER conference Academic Science and Entrepreneurship* , pp. 1-37.

Kleinknecht, A., van Montfort, K., & Brouwer, E. (2002). The non-trivial choice between innovation indicators. *Economics of Innovation and New Technologies, Vol 11, No. 2* , pp. 109-121.

Konrad, A., & Zloczysti, P. (2010). *Normung und Innovation sind keine Gegensätze.* Berlin: DIW. No. 40.

Koschatzky, K. (2001). *Räumliche Aspekte im Innovationsprozess.* Hamburg: LIT Verlag.

Kowalski, J. S., & Schaffer, A. (2011). *KIT - Impulsgeber für Karlsruhe und die TechnologieRegion.* Karlsruhe: KIT Publishing.

Lendel, I. (2010). The Impact of Research Universities on Regional Economies: The Concept of University Products. *Economic Development Quarterly, Vol 24, No. 3* , pp. 210-230.

Lepori, B., Barré, R., & Filliatreau, G. (2008). New perspectives and challenges for the design and production of S&T indicators. *Research Evaluation, Vol. 17, No. 1* , pp. 33-44.

List, F. (1841). *The National System of Political Economy.* London: Longman, English Edition 1904.

Lööf, H., & Broström, A. (2004). Does knowledge diffusion between university and industry increase innovativeness? *CESIS Electronic Working Paper Series No. 21* , pp. 1-28.

Lucas, R. (1988). On the Mechanics of Economic Development. *Journal of Monetary, Vol. 22, 2988* , pp. 3-42.

Lundvall, B.-A. (1992). *National Systems of Innovation: Towards a Theory of Innovation and Interactive Learning.* London: Pinter.

MacPherson, A. (2005). The contribution of academic-industry interaction to product innovation: The case of New York State's medical devices sector. *Regional Science, Vol. 81, Is. 1* , pp. 121-129.

Mallon, W. (2006). The Benefits and Challenges of Research Centers and Institutes in Academic Medicine: Findings from Six Universities and Their Medical Schools. *Academic Medicine, Vol. 81, No. 6* , pp. 502-512.

Mansfield, E. (1998). Academic research and industrial innovation: an update of empirical findings Research Policy 26, 773–776. *Research Policy, Vol. 26* , pp. 773–776.

Mansfield, E. (1995). Academic research underlying industrial innovations: sources, characteristics, and financing. *Review of Economics and Statistics, Vol. 77* , pp. 55–65.

Mansfield, E., & Lee, J.-Y. (1996). The modern university: contributor to industrial innovation and recipient of industrial R&D support. *Research Policy, Vol. 25* , pp. 1047-1058.

Marshall, A. (1907). *Principles of Economics.* London: Macmillan.

Martin, B., & Nightingale, P. (2000). *Science, technology and innovation.* Cheltenham.

Maurseth, P. B., & Verspagen, B. (1999). Europe: one or several systems of innovation? An analysis based on patent citations. *Open Access publications from Maastricht University* , pp. 149-174.

McKelvey, M., Alm, H., & Riccaboni, M. (2003). Does co-location matter for formal knowledge collaboration in the Swedish biotechnology–pharmaceutical sector? *Research Policy, Vol. 32, No. 3* , pp. 483-501.

Meyer-Krahmer, F., & Schmoch, U. (1998). Science-based technologie: university-industry interactions in four fields. *Research Policy, Vol. 27* , pp. 835-851.

Miner, A., Eesley, D., Devaughn, M., & Rura, T. (2001). *The Magic Beanstalk Vison: Commercialising University Inventions and Research.* Stanford: University Press.

Miozzo, M., & Dewick, P. (2004). Networks and Innovation: sustainable technologies in Scottish social housing. *R&D Management, Vol. 34, No. 3* , pp. 323-333.

Misera, S. (2010). Dirttmittelforschung - Chancen, Risiken und Praxisprobleme. Bonn: Dissertation durch die Rechts- und Staatswissenschaftliche Fakultät der Rheinischen Friedrich-Wilhelm Universität Bonn.

Monjon, S., & Waelbroeck, P. (2003). Assessing spillovers from universities to firms: evidence from French firm-level data. *International Journal of Industrial Organization, Elsevier, Vol. 21, No. 9* , pp. 1255-1270.

Morgan, K. (2004). The exaggerated death of geography: learning, proximity and territorial innovation systems. *Journal of Economic Geography, Vol. 4* , pp. 3-21.

Mowery, D., Oxley, J., & Silverman, B. (1998). Technology overlap and interfirm cooperation: implications for the resource-based view of the firm. *Research Policy, Vol. 27, No. 5* , pp. 507–523.

Mueller, P. (2006). Exploring the knowledge filter: How entrepreneurship and university-industry relationships drive economic growth. *Reserach Policy, Vol. 35* , pp. 1499-1508.

Nelson, R. (1993). *National Innovation Systems: A Comparative Analysis.* Oxford, New York, Toronto: Oxford University Press.

Niosi, J. (2002). National systems of innovations are “x-efficient” (and x-effective) Why some are slow learners. *Research Policy Vol. 31* , pp. 291–302.

Nonaka, I., & Takeuchi, H. (1995). The Knowledge-Creating Company: How Japanese Companies Create the Dynamics of Innovation. *Working Paper* , pp. 1-12.

Nooy, d. W., Mrvar, A., & Btagelj, V. (2005). *Exploratory Social Network Analysis with Pajek.* Cambridge: Cambridge Univeristy Press.

OECD. (1997). *The Measurement of Scientific and Technological Activities Oslo Manual:Guidelines for Collecting and Interpreting Innovation Data.* http://www.oecd.org/science/innovationinsciencetechnologyandindustry/2367580.pdf, 28.08.2012: Organisation for Economic Co-operation and Development, European Commission, Eurostat.

OECD. (2005). *The Measurement of Scientific and Technological Activities Oslo Manual:Guidelines for Collecting and Interpreting Innovation Data, 3rd Edition.* http://www.eds-destatis.de/downloads/publ/ISBN-92-64-01308-3.pdf, 28.08.2012: Organisation for Economic Co-operation and Development.

Oxford, U. (2012). *Oxford Dictionaries*. Retrieved from http://oxforddictionaries.com/definition/english/knowledge?q=knowledge, 28.08.2012

Patel, P., & Pavitt, K. (1997). The technological competencies of the world' s largest firms:complex and path-dependent, but not much variety. *Research Policy VOl. 26* , pp. 141-156.

Plotkin, H. (1994). *The Nature of Knowledge: Concerning Adaptations, Instinct and the Evolution of Intelligence.* London: Allen Lane.

Polanyi, M. (1958). *Personal Knowledge: Towards a Post-critical Philosophy.* London: Routledge and Kegan Paul.

Porter, M. E. (2000). Location, Competition, and Economic Development: Local Clusters in a Global Economy. *Economic Development Quartely, Vol. 14, No. 1* , pp. 15-34.

Portes, A., & Sensenbrenner, J. (1993). Embeddedness and Immigration: Notes on the Social Determinants of Economic Action. *American Journal of Sociology, Vol. 98 No.6* , pp. 1320-1349.

Powell, W. (1990). Neither market nor hierarchy: Network forms of organization. *Research in Organizational Behavior, edited by Barry M. Staw and L. L. Cummings: JAI* , pp. 295–336.

Rallet, T., & Torre, A. (2000). Is geographical proximity necessary in the innovation networks in the era if global economy? *GeoJournal, Vol. 49* , pp. 373-380.

Reud, N., & Smith, B. W. (2009). Social network analysis: Its use in local economic development. *Economic Development Journal* , pp. 48-55.

Reuters, T. (2012). *Web of Science*. Retrieved from http://wokinfo.com/

Roberts, E. B. (2007). Managing Invention and Innovation. *Research Technology Management, Vol. 55* , pp. 35-54.

Rogers, M. (1998). The Definition and Measurement of Innovation. *Melbourne Institute Working Paper No. 10/1998* .

Romer, P. M. (1990). Endogenous technological change. *Journal of Political Economy, 98* , pp. 71-102.

Romer, P. M. (1986). Increasing Returns and Long-run Growth. *Journal of Political Economy, Vol. 94* , pp. 1002-1037.

Rosenberg, N., & Nelson, R. (1994). American universities and technical advance in industry. *Research Policy, Vol. 23* , pp. 323–348.

Rosenberg, N., & Nelson, R. (1993). *Technical innovation and national systems.* New York: Oxford: Oxford University.

Sacchetti, S., & Sugden, R. (2003). The Governance of Networks and Economic Power: The Nature and Impact of Subcontracting Relationships. *Journal of Economic Survey, Vol. 17, No. 5* , pp. 670-691.

Schartinger, D., Rammera, C., Fischer, M. M., & Fröhlich, J. (2002). Knowledge interactions between universities and industry in Austria: sectoral patterns and determinants. *Research Policy, Vol. 31* , pp. 303–328.

Schmoch, U. (2003). *Hochschulforschung und Industrieforschung: Perspektiven der Interaktion.* Frankfurt/New York: Campus Verlag.

Schmoch, U. (1999). Interaction of Universities and Industrial Enterprises in Germany and the United States-A Comparison. *Industty and Innovation, Vol. 6, No. 1* , pp. 51-68.

Schmoch, U. (1990). *Wettbewerbsvorsprung durch Patentinformation – Handbuch für dieRecherchenpraxis.* Köln: Verlag TÜV Rheinland GmbH.

Schmoch, U., Grupp, H., & Mannsbart, W. (1988). *Technikprognosen mit Patentindikatoren* . Köln: Verlag TÜV Rheinland.

Schumpeter, J. A. (1939). *BUSINESS CYCLES - A Theoretical, Historical and Statistical Analysis of the Capitalist Process.* New York, Toronto, London: McGraw-Hill Book.

Schumpeter, J. A. (1911). *Theorie der wirtschaftlichen Entwicklung.* München und Leipzig: Neuausgabe hrgg. von Röpke, J. and Stiller, O., Berlin 2006.

Scopus. (2013). *Sciencedirect.* Retrieved from http://www.sciencedirect.com/

Scott, J. (1988). Social Network Analysis. *Sociology, Vol. 22, No. 1* , pp. 109-127.

Scott, J. (1991). *Social network analysis: A handbook.* London: Sage.

Simmie, J. (2004). Innovation and Clustering in the Globalised International Economy. *Urban Studies, Vol. 41, No. 5/6* , pp. 1095-1112.

Smith, A., & McCulloch, J. (1776). *An inquiry into the nature and causes of the wealth of nations.* Harvard College: Harvard College Library.

Solow, R. (1956). A Contribution to the Theory of Economic Growth. *The Quarterly Journal of Economics, Vol. 70, No. 1, Published by: The MIT* , pp. 65-94.

Stephan, P. E. (1996). The Economics of Science. *Journal of Economic Literature, American Economic Association, Vol. 36, No. 3* , pp. 1199-1235.

Storper, M., & Venables, A. (2004). Buzz: face-to-face contact and the urban economy. *Journal of Economic Geography, Vol. 4, Is. 4* , pp. 351-370.

Teece, D. (1992). Competition, cooperation, and innovation: organizational arrangements for regimes of rapid technological progress. *Journal of Economic Behavior and Organization, Vol. 18, No. 1* , pp. 1–25.

Tijssen, R. J. (1998). Science and Technology Indicators. *Science and Technology* , pp. 1-34.

Tijssen, R. (2002). Science dependence of technologies: evidence from inventions and their inventors. *Research Policy, Vol. 31* , pp. 509-526.

Tindall, D. B., & Wellman, B. (2001). Canada as Social Structure: Social Network Analysis and Canadian Sociology. *Canadian Journal of Sociology, Vol. 26* , pp. 265-308.

Tödtling, F., Lehner, P., & Kaufmann, A. (2009). Do different types of innovation rely on specific kinds of knowledge interactions? *Technovation Vol. 29* , pp. 59-71.

Torre, A., & Rallet, A. (2005). Proximity and Localization. *Regional Studies, Vol. 39, No. 1* , pp. 47-59.

Tran, C. A. (2011). *Role and Dynamics of ‚Late-comers' in the global Technology Competition.* Karlsruhe: KIT Scientific Publishing.

Trune, D. R., & Gosling, L. N. (1998). University Technology Transfer Programs: A Profit/Loss Analysis. *Technological Forecasting and Social Change, Vol. 57, No. 3* , pp. 197–204.

Vahs, D., & Burmester, R. (2002). *Innovationsmanagement: von der Produktidee zur erfolgreichen Vermarktung.* Stuttgart: Schaffer und Poeschel Verlag, 2. Auflage.

Von Hippel, E. (1988). *The Sources of Innovation.* New York: Oxford University Press.

Wainfan, L., & Davis, P. K. (2004). *Challenges in Virtual Collaboration: Videoconferencing, Audioconferencing, and Computer-Mediated Communications.* Pittsburgh: RAND.

Wasserman, S., & Faust, K. (1994). *Social Network Analysis: Methods and Applications.* Cambridge: Cambridge University Press.

Web of Knowledge. (2012). Retrieved from http://apps.webofknowledge.com/WOS_GeneralSearch_input.do?product=WOS&SID=T1iiAmOHI4olEmfFi85&search_mode=GeneralSearch

Wissenschaftsrat. (2007). *Empfehlungen zur Interaktion von Wissenschaft und Wirtschaft.* http://www.wissenschaftsrat.de/download/archiv/7901-07.pdf, 07.09.2012.

Xu, J., & Chen, H. (2005). Criminal network analysis and visualisation. *Communications of the ACM, Vol. 48, Iss. 6* , pp. 100-107.

Zißler, M. (2011). *Technologietransfer durch Auftragsforschung.* Wiesbaden: Gabler Verlag.

Zucker, L., & Darby, M. R. (2001). Capturing Technological Opportunity via Japan's Star Scientists: Evidence from Japanese Firms' Biotech Patents and Products. *The Journal of Technology Transfer, Vol. 26, No. 1-2* , pp. 37-58.

14. Appendix

Appendix 1: Overview of all German universities that are subject of study (own illustration).

Overview of all German Univeristies that are Subject of Study									
German Univeristies	Actors-Code	Elite University	Medical University	Technical University	German Univeristies	Actors-Code	Elite University	Medical University	Technical University
Aachen RWTH	11	x	x	x	Hildesheim	65			
Augsburg	19				Hohenheim	72			
Bamberg	20				Ilmenau	86			x
Bayreuth	21		x		Jena	87		x	
Berlin FU	75	x	x		Kaiserslautern	38		x	x
Berlin HU	76	x	x		Kassel	39			
Berlin TU	77			x	Kiel	40		x	
Bielefeld	22		x		KIT	10	x		x
Bochum	23		x		Koblenz Landau	41		x	
Bonn	24				Köln	43	x	x	
Braunschweig	25			x	Konstanz	17	x		
Bremen	26	x	x		Leipzig	88		x	
Chemnitz	78			x	Lübeck	67		x	
Clausthal	61			x	Lüneburg	68			
Cottbus	79			x	Magdeburg	89		x	
Darmstadt	28			x	Mainz	44		x	
Dortmund	29			x	Mannheim	45			
Dresden	80	x	x	x	Marburg	46		x	
Duisburg Essen	30		x		München [federal armed forces]	70			x
Düsseldorf	31		x		München LMU	12	x	x	
Eichstätt Ingolstadt	66				München TU	13	x	x	x
Erfurt	81				Münster	47		x	
Erlangen Nürnberg	32		x		Oldenburg	48			
Flensburg	62		x		Osnabrück	49		x	
Frankfurt	33		x		Paserborn	50			
Frankfurt Oder	82				Passau	51			
Freiberg	83			x	Potsdam	90			
Freiburg	16	x	x		Regensburg	52		x	
Gießen	34		x		Rostock	91		x	
Göttingen	15	x	x		Saarbrücken	53		x	
Greifswald	84		x		Siegen	54			
Hagen	35				Stuttgart	55			x
Halle Wittenberg	85		x		Trier	56			
Hamburg	36		x		Tübingen	57	x	x	
Hamburg [federal armed forces]	63		x		Ulm	58		x	
Hamburg Harburg	64			x	Weimar	92			
Hannover	37		x	x	Wuppertal	59			
Heidelberg	14	x	x		Würzburg	60		x	

Appendix 2: PATSTATT IWW Data-Base

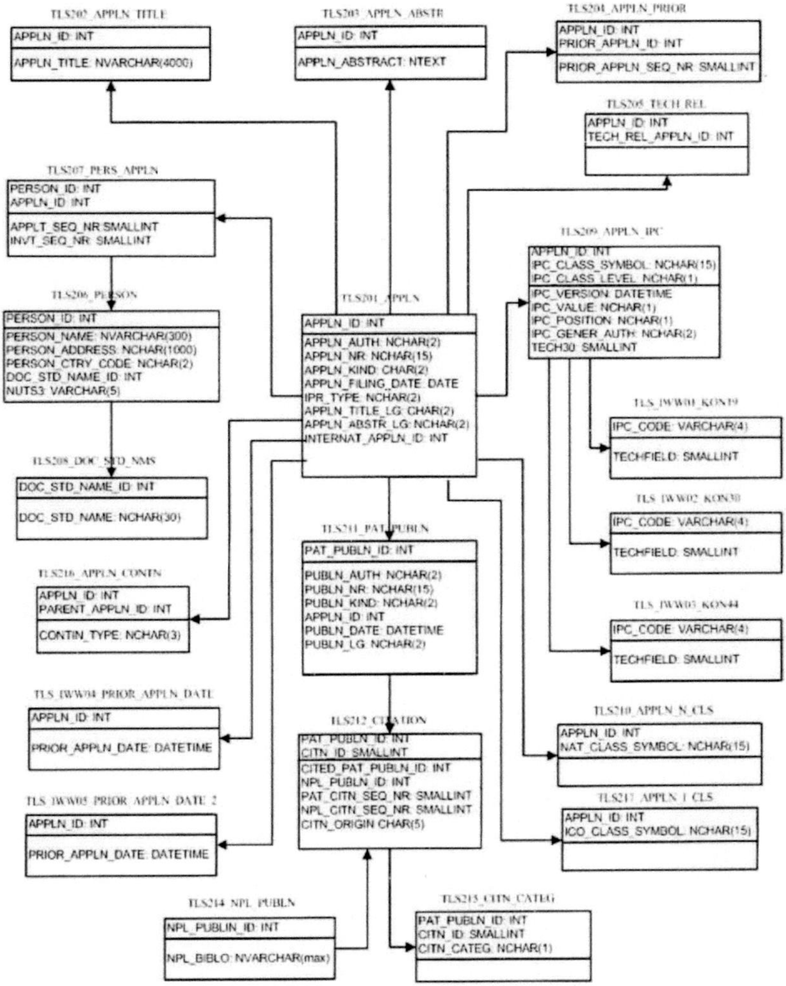
TLS202_APPLN_TITLE
APPLN_ID: INT
APPLN_TITLE: NVARCHAR(4000)
TLS203_APPLN_ABSTR
APPLN_ID: INT
APPLN_ABSTRACT: NTEXT
TLS204_APPLN_PRIOR
APPLN_ID: INT
PRIOR_APPLN_ID: INT
PRIOR_APPLN_SEQ_NR: SMALLINT
TLS205_TECH_REL
APPLN_ID: INT
TECH_REL_APPLN_ID: INT
TLS207_PERS_APPLN
PERSON_ID: INT
APPLN_ID: INT
APPLT_SEQ_NR:SMALLINT
INVT_SEQ_NR: SMALLINT
TLS209_APPLN_IPC
APPLN_ID: INT
IPC_CLASS_SYMBOL: NCHAR(15)
IPC_CLASS_LEVEL: NCHAR(1)
IPC_VERSION: DATETIME
IPC_VALUE: NCHAR(1)
IPC_POSITION: NCHAR(1)
IPC_GENER_AUTH: NCHAR(2)
TECH30: SMALLINT
TLS206_PERSON
PERSON_ID: INT
PERSON_NAME: NVARCHAR(300)
PERSON_ADDRESS: NCHAR(1000)
PERSON_CTRY_CODE: NCHAR(2)
DOC_STD_NAME_ID: INT
NUTS3: VARCHAR(5)
TLS201_APPLN
APPLN_ID: INT
APPLN_AUTH: NCHAR(2)
APPLN_NR: NCHAR(15)
APPLN_KIND: CHAR(2)
APPLN_FILING_DATE: DATE
IPR_TYPE: NCHAR(2)
APPLN_TITLE_LG: CHAR(2)
APPLN_ABSTR_LG: NCHAR(2)
INTERNAT_APPLN_ID: INT
TLS_IWW01_KON19
IPC_CODE: VARCHAR(4)
TECHFIELD: SMALLINT
TLS208_DOC_STD_NMS
DOC_STD_NAME_ID: INT
DOC_STD_NAME: NCHAR(30)
TLS_IWW02_KON30
IPC_CODE: VARCHAR(4)
TECHFIELD: SMALLINT
TLS211_PAT_PUBLN
PAT_PUBLN_ID: INT
PUBLN_AUTH: NCHAR(2)
PUBLN_NR: NCHAR(15)
PUBLN_KIND: NCHAR(2)
APPLN_ID: INT
PUBLN_DATE: DATETIME
PUBLN_LG: NCHAR(2)
TLS216_APPLN_CONTN
APPLN_ID: INT
PARENT_APPLN_ID: INT
CONTIN_TYPE: NCHAR(3)
TLS_IWW03_KON44
IPC_CODE: VARCHAR(4)
TECHFIELD: SMALLINT
TLS_IWW04_PRIOR_APPLN_DATE
APPLN_ID: INT
PRIOR_APPLN_DATE: DATETIME
TLS212_CITATION
PAT_PUBLN_ID: INT
CITN_ID: SMALLINT
CITED_PAT_PUBLN_ID: INT
NPL_PUBLN_ID: INT
PAT_CITN_SEQ_NR: SMALLINT
NPL_CITN_SEQ_NR: SMALLINT
CITN_ORIGIN: CHAR(5)
TLS210_APPLN_N_CLS
APPLN_ID: INT
NAT_CLASS_SYMBOL: NCHAR(15)
TLS_IWW05_PRIOR_APPLN_DATE_2
APPLN_ID: INT
PRIOR_APPLN_DATE: DATETIME
TLS217_APPLN_I_CLS
APPLN_ID: INT
ICO_CLASS_SYMBOL: NCHAR(15)
TLS214_NPL_PUBLN
NPL_PUBLIN_ID: INT
NPL_BIBLO: NVARCHAR(max)
TLS215_CITN_CATEG
PAT_PUBLN_ID: INT
CITN_ID: SMALLINT
CITN_CATEG: NCHAR(1)

Appendix 3: Exemplary Illustration of calculating the different Distances between the German Universities and their individual Cooperation Partners using the Haversine Formula.

```
Sub abstand()
Application.ScreenUpdating = False
Dim Ende As Long
Ende = 280000

Dim step As Long
step = 0
For gesamt = 10 To 92



Dim Uniname(92) As String

Uniname(1) = "Forschungszentrum"
Uniname(2) = "Unternehmen"
Uniname(10) = "kit"
Uniname(11) = "rwth aachen"
Uniname(12) = "lmu"
Uniname(13) = "münchen th"
Uniname(14) = "uni heidelberg"
Uniname(15) = "uni göttingen"
Uniname(16) = "uni freiburg"
Uniname(17) = "uni konstanz"
Uniname(19) = "uni augsburg"
Uniname(20) = "uni bamberg"
Uniname(21) = "uni bayreuth"
Uniname(22) = "uni bielefeld"
Uniname(23) = "uni bochum"
Uniname(24) = "uni bonn"
Uniname(25) = "braunschweig tu"
Uniname(26) = "uni bremen"
Uniname(28) = "darmstadt tu"
Uniname(29) = "dortmund tu"
Uniname(30) = "uni duisburg essen"
Uniname(31) = "uni düsseldorf"
Uniname(32) = "uni erlangen nürnberg"
Uniname(33) = "uni frankfurt"
Uniname(34) = "uni gießen"
Uniname(35) = "fernuni hagen"
```

```
Uniname(36)  = "uni hamburg"
Uniname(37)  = "uni hannover"
Uniname(38)  = "kaiserslautern tu"
Uniname(39)  = "uni kassel"
Uniname(40)  = "uni kiel"
Uniname(41)  = "uni koblenz-landau"
Uniname(43)  = "uni köln"
Uniname(44)  = "uni mainz"
Uniname(45)  = "uni mannheim"
Uniname(46)  = "uni marburg"
Uniname(47)  = "uni münster"
Uniname(48)  = "uni oldenburg"
Uniname(49)  = "uni osnabrück"
Uniname(50)  = "uni paderborn"
Uniname(51)  = "uni passau"
Uniname(52)  = "uni regensburg"
Uniname(53)  = "uni des saarlandes"
Uniname(54)  = "uni siegen"
Uniname(55)  = "uni stuttgart"
Uniname(56)  = "uni trier"
Uniname(57)  = "uni tübingen"
Uniname(58)  = "uni Ulm"
Uniname(59)  = "uni wuppertal"
Uniname(60)  = "uni würzburg"
Uniname(61)  = "TU Clausthal"
Uniname(62)  = "Uni Flensburg"
Uniname(63)  = "Bundeswehr Hamburg"
Uniname(64)  = "Uni Hamburg Harburg"
Uniname(65)  = "Uni Hildesheim"
Uniname(66)  = "Uni Eichstädt Ingolstadt"
Uniname(67)  = "Uni Lübeck"
Uniname(68)  = "Uni Lüneburg"
Uniname(69)  = "Uni Mannheim"
Uniname(70)  = "Uni Bundeswehr München"
Uniname(71)  = "Uni Passau"
Uniname(72)  = "Uni Hohenheim"
Uniname(75)  = "Freie Uni Berlin"
Uniname(76)  = "Humboldt Uni Berlin "
Uniname(77)  = "TU Berlin"
Uniname(78)  = "TU Chemnitz"
Uniname(79)  = "TU Cottbus"
Uniname(80)  = "TU Dresden"
Uniname(81)  = "Uni Erfurt"
Uniname(82)  = "Uni Frankfurt Oder"
Uniname(83)  = "TU Bergakademie Freiberg"
Uniname(84)  = "uni Greifswald"
Uniname(85)  = "uni halle-wittenberg"
Uniname(86)  = "tu ilmenau"
```

```
Uniname(87) = "friedrich schiller uni jena"
Uniname(88) = "uni leipzig"
Uniname(89) = "uni magdeburg"
Uniname(90) = "uni potsdam"
Uniname(91) = "uni rostock"
Uniname(92) = "bauhaus uni weimar"

If Uniname(gesamt) <> "" Then

Dim abstand As Double
Dim abstandh As Double
Dim platz As Long
Dim uni As Integer
Dim entf(40) As Long
Dim entfg(40) As Double
Dim dabei As Boolean
Dim ausland As Long
Dim arg As Double
Dim Eigengewicht As Double
Eigengewicht = 0

For i = 1 To 40
entf(i) = 0
Next
For ii = 1 To 40
entfg(ii) = 0
Next
ausland = 0
uni = gesamt
Dim gewichtungscount As Long

For Z = 2 To Ende
 dabei = False
 gewichtungscount = 0
 For X = 1 To 500
  If Cells(Z + X - 1, 9) = uni Then
   dabei = True
   platz = X
   Eigengewicht = Eigengewicht + Cells(Z + X - 1, 8).Value
  End If
  If Cells(Z + X - 1, 9) > 6 Then
  gewichtungscount = gewichtungscount + 1
  End If
  If Cells(Z + X - 1, 1) <> Cells(Z + X, 1) Then
  Exit For
  End If
 Next
 If dabei = True Then
```

```
 For Count = 1 To X
  If Count <> platz And Cells(Z + Count - 1, 13) <> "" Then
   'abstand = (((Cells(Z + count - 1, 13) - Cells(Z + platz
- 1, 13)) * 71.46) ^ 2 + ((Cells(Z + count - 1, 14) -
Cells(Z + platz - 1, 14)) * 111) ^ 2) ^ (0.5)
   arg = Sqr((Sin((Cells(Z + Count - 1, 14) / 180 *
3.1415926 - Cells(Z + platz - 1, 14) / 180 * 3.1415926) /
2)) ^ 2 + Cos(Cells(Z + platz - 1, 14) / 180 * 3.1415926) *
Cos(Cells(Z + Count - 1, 14) / 180 * 3.1415926) *
(Sin((Cells(Z + Count - 1, 13) / 180 * 3.1415926 - Cells(Z
+ platz - 1, 13) / 180 * 3.1415926) / 2)) ^ 2)
   abstandh = 2 * 6371 * Atn(arg / Sqr(-arg * arg + 1))
   'Cells(Z + count - 1, 15) = abstand
  If abstandh > 0 And abstandh <= 25 Then
  entf(1) = entf(1) + 1
  entfg(1) = entfg(1) + Cells(Z + Count - 1, 8).Value /
gewichtungscount
  End If
  If abstandh > 25 And abstandh <= 50 Then
  entf(2) = entf(2) + 1
  entfg(2) = entfg(2) + Cells(Z + Count - 1, 8).Value /
gewichtungscount
  End If
  If abstandh > 50 And abstandh <= 75 Then
  entf(3) = entf(3) + 1
  entfg(3) = entfg(3) + Cells(Z + Count - 1, 8).Value /
gewichtungscount
  End If
  If abstandh > 75 And abstandh <= 100 Then
  entf(4) = entf(4) + 1
  entfg(4) = entfg(4) + Cells(Z + Count - 1, 8).Value /
gewichtungscount
  End If
  End If
  'If count <> platz And (Cells(Z + count - 1, 3) <> "de"
And Cells(Z + X - 1, 3) <> "De") Then
  'ausland = ausland + 1
  'End If
  'If Cells(Z + count - 1, 14) <> "" Then
  'Cells(Z + count - 1, 15) = abstand
  'Cells(Z + count - 1, 16) = abstandh
  'Cells(Z + count - 1, 17) = arg
  'End If
 Next
 End If
 Z = Z + X - 1

Next
```

```
For j = 1 To 40
Cells(j + 1, 17 + 4 * step) = entf(j)
Next
For jj = 1 To 40
Cells(jj + 1, 18 + 4 * step) = entfg(jj)
Next
 Dim Namee(2) As String
 Namee(1) = "Ergebnis "
 Namee(2) = Uniname(uni)


Cells(1, 16 + 4 * step) = Join(Namee)
'Cells(7, 17 + 4 * step) = ausland
Cells(2, 16 + 4 * step) = "25km"
Cells(3, 16 + 4 * step) = "25-50km"
Cells(4, 16 + 4 * step) = "50-75km"
Cells(5, 16 + 4 * step) = "75-100km"
Cells(8, 16 + 4 * step) = "Eigengewicht"
Cells(8, 17 + 4 * step) = Eigengewicht

step = step + 1
End If
Next
End Sub
```

Appendix 4: Value of normalized Degree Centrality regarding the Publication Activity of all German Universities in 2000 and compared by Ranking to 2009 (own illustration).

Value of normalized Degree Centrality regarding the Publication Activity of all German Universities in 2000 and compared by Ranking to 2009							
Rank 2000	Value of normalised Degree-Centrality	Rank 2009	German University	Rank 2000	Value of normalised Degree-Centrality	Rank 2009	German University
1.	0.0686100	2	MÜNCHEN TU	39.	0.0150353	40	BRAUNSCHWEIG
2.	0.0674440	3	MÜNCHEN LMU	40.	0.0148819	27	BREMEN
3.	0.0643142	1	HEIDELBERG	41.	0.0145443	32	DORTMUND
4.	0.0555385	7	KIT	42.	0.0140841	48	KONSTANZ
5.	0.0548328	5	HAMBURG	43.	0.0129488	37	LÜBECK
6.	0.0496164	4	BONN	44.	0.0120896	34	ROSTOCK
7.	0.0471617	6	FREIBURG	45.	0.0098496	54	OSNABRÜCK
8.	0.0467628	13	RWTH	46.	0.0097269	43	POTSDAM
9.	0.0423750	10	TÜBINGEN	47.	0.0095735	51	KAISERSLAUTERN
10.	0.0396134	17	MAINZ	48.	0.0093587	41	SAARBRÜCKEN
11.	0.0394600	24	BERLIN	49.	0.0088984	46	MAGDEBURG
12.	0.0388770	9	ERLANGEN-Nürnberg	50.	0.0080700	52	HOHENHEIM
13.	0.0370359	12	HANNOVER	51.	0.0079779	56	PADERBORN
14.	0.0358085	24	BERLIN	52.	0.0069960	57	CHEMNITZ
15.	0.0345505	8	KÖLN	53.	0.0068119	63	FREIBERG
16.	0.0332004	18	WÜRZBURG	54.	0.0065664	44	GREIFSWALD
17.	0.0310525	14	GÖTTINGEN	55.	0.0063823	59	CLAUSTHAL
18.	0.0301933	23	DUISBURG ESSEN	56.	0.0061369	58	KASSEL
19.	0.0298865	20	BOCHUM	57.	0.0058607	55	AUGSBURG
20.	0.0297637	15	MÜNSTER	58.	0.0057686	30	HAGEN
21.	0.0297637	16	ULM	59.	0.0047561	49	MANNHEIM
22.	0.0293648	19	KIEL	60.	0.0039583	53	OLDENBURG
23.	0.0275545	22	LEIPZIG	61.	0.0038355	60	ILMENAU
24.	0.0256214	33	STUTTGART	62.	0.0027309	61	HAMBURG HARBURG
25.	0.0249770	24	BERLIN	63.	0.0021479	62	TRIER
26.	0.0233507	11	DRESDEN	64.	0.0019331	66	COTTBUS
27.	0.0213869	35	DARMSTADT	65.	0.0011967	67	MÜNCHEN BUNDESWEHR
28.	0.0209267	25	REGENSBURG	66.	0.0010739	75	HAMBURG BUNDESWEHR
29.	0.0200675	21	FRANKFURT	67.	0.0007671	72	ERFURT
30.	0.0196993	38	MARBURG	68.	0.0005216	70	PASSAU
31.	0.0194538	39	WUPPERTAL	69.	0.0003682	64	KOBLENZ LANDAU
32.	0.0188708	47	BAYREUTH	70.	0.0003375	65	BAMBERG
33.	0.0186253	31	JENA	71.	0.0001841	71	EICHSTÄTT INGOLSTADT
34.	0.0174287	26	DÜSSELDORF	72.	0.0001731	74	FRANKFURT ODER
35.	0.0169684	28	GIESSEN	73.	0.0001534	69	WEIMAR
36.	0.0166922	42	HALLE WITTENBERG	74.	0.0000614	73	HILDESHEIM
37.	0.0151580	45	BIELEFELD	75.	0.0000000	76	FLENSBURG
38.	0.0150660	50	SIEGEN	76.	0.0000000	68	LÜNEBURG

Appendix 5: Value of Betweenness-Centrality regarding the Publication Activity of all German Universities in 2000 and compared by Ranking to 2009 (own illustration).

Value Betweenness-Centrality regarding the Publication Activity of all German Universities in 2000 and compared by Ranking to 2009

Rank	Betweenness Centrality	Rank 2009	German University	Rank	Betweenness Centrality	Rank 2009	German University
1.	0.0887127	2.	MÜNCHEN TU	39.	0.0184719	35.	BRAUNSCHWEIG
2.	0.0868062	3.	MÜNCHEN LMU	40.	0.0175382	42.	DORTMUND
3.	0.0854576	1.	HEIDELBERG	41.	0.0170603	34.	ROSTOCK
4.	0.0757067	5.	KIT	42.	0.0159328	41.	LÜBECK
5.	0.0646542	6.	HAMBURG	43.	0.0150295	55.	OSNABRÜCK
6.	0.0618062	12.	TÜBINGEN	44.	0.0144612	48.	WUPPERTAL
7.	0.0601411	4.	BONN	45.	0.0134701	50.	KAISERSLAUTERN
8.	0.0578630	14.	RWTH	46.	0.0131065	36.	POTSDAM
9.	0.0572415	10.	HANNOVER	47.	0.0115210	49.	HOHENHEIM
10.	0.0566769	9.	ERLANGEN NÜRNBERG	48.	0.0112244	39.	SAARBRÜCKEN
11.	0.0556800	29.	BERLIN FU	49.	0.0099480	56.	PADERBORN
12.	0.0549117	8.	FREIBURG	50.	0.0094297	54.	CHEMNITZ
13.	0.0498451	18.	WÜRZBURG	51.	0.0093490	62.	FREIBERG
14.	0.0486494	7.	KÖLN	52.	0.0091096	46.	MAGDEBURG
15.	0.0485034	30.	BERLIN HU	53.	0.0090650	51.	SIEGEN
16.	0.0462799	19.	DUISBURG ESSEN	54.	0.0089561	59.	KASSEL
17.	0.0458022	22.	MAINZ	55.	0.0080638	58.	CLAUSTHAL
18.	0.0447999	13.	GÖTTINGEN	56.	0.0076892	47.	GREIFSWALD
19.	0.0435373	21.	BOCHUM	57.	0.0055399	57.	AUGSBURG
20.	0.0434656	16.	ULM	58.	0.0053960	53.	MANNHEIM
21.	0.0422583	17.	LEIPZIG	59.	0.0048402	45.	HAGEN
22.	0.0409246	20.	KIEL	60.	0.0048113	60.	ILMENAU
23.	0.0408345	15.	MÜNSTER	61.	0.0040871	52.	OLDENBURG
24.	0.0405955	27.	STUTTGART	62.	0.0033357	61.	HAMBURG HARBURG
25.	0.0367444	24.	BERLIN TU	63.	0.0021442	63.	TRIER
26.	0.0351199	11.	DRESDEN	64.	0.0021010	65.	COTTBUS
27.	0.0324799	31.	DARMSTADT	65.	0.0012930	68.	MÜNCHEN BUNDESWEHR
28.	0.0281063	26.	REGENSBURG	66.	0.0005167	70.	PASSAU
29.	0.0277476	40.	BAYREUTH	67.	0.0004781	75.	HAMBURG BUNDESWEHR
30.	0.0273388	28.	JENA	68.	0.0003759	73.	ERFURT
31.	0.0261111	38.	MARBURG	69.	0.0002365	64.	KOBLENZ LANDAU
32.	0.0253938	25.	FRANKFURT	70.	0.0001401	66.	BAMBERG
33.	0.0231299	37.	HALLE WITTENBERG	71.	0.0001315	72.	EICHSTÄTT INGOLSTADT
34.	0.0228289	33.	DÜSSELDORF	72.	0.0001285	71.	FRANKFURT ODER
35.	0.0222488	32.	GIESSEN	73.	0.0001227	69.	WEIMAR
36.	0.0219066	23.	BREMEN	74.	0.0000614	74.	HILDESHEIM
37.	0.0215150	44.	KONSTANZ	75.	0.0000000	76.	FLENSBURG
38.	0.0213331	43.	BIELEFELD	76.	0.0000000	67.	LÜNEBURG

Appendix 6: Value of normalized Degree Centrality regarding the Patenting Activity of all German Universities (Ranking) 2007/2008 (own illustration).

Normalized Degree Centrality of all German Universities, 2007/2008					
Rank	Normalized Degree Centrality	German University	Rank	Normalized Degree Centrality	German University
1.	0.0608696	ERLANGEN-NÜRNBERG	32.	0.0086957	PADERBORN
2.	0.0608696	WÜRZBURG	33.	0.0086957	STUTTGART
3.	0.0521739	KIT	34.	0.0086957	ULM
4.	0.0405797	FREIBURG	35.	0.0086957	SAARBRÜCKEN
5.	0.0376812	HAMBURG	36.	0.0086957	KASSEL
6.	0.0347826	MÜNCHEN	37.	0.0057971	HANNOVER
7.	0.0318841	DRESDEN	38.	0.0057971	KONSTANZ
8.	0.0260870	AACHEN	39.	0.0057971	KIEL
9.	0.0260870	MÜNCHEN	40.	0.0057971	BREMEN
10.	0.0231884	DUISBURG-ESSEN	41.	0.0028986	CHEMNITZ
11.	0.0231884	ROSTOCK	42.	0.0028986	MARBURG
12.	0.0231884	GÖTTINGEN	43.	0.0028986	TÜBINGEN
13.	0.0202899	JENA	44.	0.0028986	BAMBERG
14.	0.0202899	DÜSSELDORF	45.	0.0028986	REGENSBURG
15.	0.0173913	BERLIN FU	46.	0.0028986	LÜBECK
16.	0.0173913	MAINZ	47.	0.0028986	OLDENBURG
17.	0.0173913	BRAUNSCHWEIG	48.	0.0028986	FREIBERG
18.	0.0173913	KAISERSLAUTERN	49.	0.0028986	GIESSEN
19.	0.0173913	BONN	50.	0.0028986	MAGDEBURG
20.	0.0173913	ILMENAU	51.	0.0028986	CLAUSTHAL
21.	0.0144928	HEIDELBERG	52.	0.0028986	SIEGEN
22.	0.0144928	BERLIN TU	53.	0.0000000	DORTMUND
23.	0.0144928	MÜNSTER	54.	0.0000000	BAYREUTH
24.	0.0144928	KÖLN	55.	0.0000000	BUNDESWEHR Hamburg
25.	0.0144928	FRANKFURT	56.	0.0000000	OSNABRÜCK
26.	0.0115942	BERLIN HUMBOLDT	57.	0.0000000	HOHENHEIM
27.	0.0115942	HAMBURG-HARBURG	58.	0.0000000	LEIPZIG
28.	0.0115942	BOCHUM	59.	0.0000000	POTSDAM
29.	0.0115942	GREIFSWALD	60.	0.0000000	COTTBUS
30.	0.0115942	BIELEFELD	61.	0.0000000	WUPPERTAL
31.	0.0086957	PADERBORN	62.	0.0000000	DARMSTADT

Appendix 7: Value of Betweenness Centrality regarding the Patenting Activity of all German Universities (Ranking) 2007/2008 (own illustration).

Betweenness Centrality of all German Universities, 2007/2008

Rank	Betweenness Centrality	German University	Rank	Betweenness Centrality	German University
1.	0.1150640	KIT	32.	0.0057526	BOCHUM
2.	0.0896877	ERLANGEN-NÜRNBERG	33.	0.0046781	SAARBRÜCKEN
3.	0.0652174	MÜNCHEN	34.	0.0036906	KONSTANZ
4.	0.0596899	WÜRZBURG	35.	0.0036906	CHEMNITZ
5.	0.0512122	FREIBURG	36.	0.0036906	KAISERSLAUTERN
6.	0.0434592	AACHEN	37.	0.0036906	HANNOVER
7.	0.0396224	HAMBURG	38.	0.0001180	MÜNSTER
8.	0.0362508	MÜNCHEN	39.	0.0000169	KIEL
9.	0.0360527	DÜSSELDORF	40.	0.0000000	MARBURG
10.	0.0331423	GÖTTINGEN	41.	0.0000000	BREMEN
11.	0.0304385	DUISBURG-ESSEN	42.	0.0000000	TÜBINGEN
12.	0.0294844	DRESDEN	43.	0.0000000	BAYREUTH
13.	0.0251563	ROSTOCK	44.	0.0000000	BUNDESWEHR HAMBURG
14.	0.0247800	JENA	45.	0.0000000	OSNABRÜCK
15.	0.0217897	BRAUNSCHWEIG	46.	0.0000000	BAMBERG
16.	0.0185988	BERLIN FU	47.	0.0000000	HOHENHEIM
17.	0.0166924	MAINZ	48.	0.0000000	REGENSBURG
18.	0.0143471	FRANKFURT	49.	0.0000000	LEIPZIG
19.	0.0120356	BERLIN TU	50.	0.0000000	POTSDAM
20.	0.0110297	BONN	51.	0.0000000	LÜBECK
21.	0.0109707	BIELEFELD	52.	0.0000000	COTTBUS
22.	0.0102194	BERLIN HUMBOLDT	53.	0.0000000	OLDENBURG
23.	0.0100627	HEIDELBERG	54.	0.0000000	FREIBERG
24.	0.0075848	ILMENAU	55.	0.0000000	WUPPERTAL
25.	0.0073643	PADERBORN	56.	0.0000000	GIESSEN
26.	0.0073643	STUTTGART	57.	0.0000000	MAGDEBURG
27.	0.0073643	ULM	58.	0.0000000	CLAUSTHAL
28.	0.0073643	KASSEL	59.	0.0000000	SIEGEN
29.	0.0073643	GREIFSWALD	60.	0.0000000	DORTMUND
30.	0.0073475	HAMBURG-HARBURG	61.	0.0000000	DARMSTADT
31.	0.0072688	KÖLN			

Appendix 8: Overview of Publication Activity of all German Universities in absolute Numbers, 2000 (own illustration).

Overview of Publication Activity of all German Universities in absolute Numbers, 2000 (Differences in Size are not considered)					
University	Single-Authorship	Co-Authorship	University	Single-Authorship	Co-Authorship
Aachen RWTH	832	799	Hildesheim	3	2
Augsburg	82	148	Hohenheim	151	162
Bamberg	17	9	Ilmenau	44	84
Bayreuth	220	403	Jena	389	463
Berlin FU	544	956	Kaiserslautern	214	208
Berlin Humboldt	585	904	Kassel	104	123
Berlin TU	387	601	Kiel	452	520
Bielefeld	256	293	KIT	700	831
Bochum	511	643	Koblenz-Landau	15	9
Bonn	625	934	Köln	666	735
Braunschweig	238	287	Konstanz	204	289
Bremen	284	311	Leipzig	499	662
Chemnitz	102	172	Lübeck	352	251
Clausthal	85	121	Lüneburg	2	0
Cottbus	43	45	Magdeburg	138	216
Darmstadt	355	440	Mainz	409	615
Dortmund	299	282	Mannheim	119	113
Dresden	489	517	Marburg	344	460
Duisburg-Essen	567	566	München Bundeswehr	54	27
Düsseldorf	304	400	München LMU	835	1166
Eichstädt-Ingolstadt	14	6	München TU	930	1257
Erfurt	2	18	Münster	597	594
Erlangen-Nürnberg	753	809	Oldenburg	115	96
Flensburg	1	0	Osnabrück	129	204
Frankfurt	284	392	Paderborn	130	154
Frankfurt Oder	17	6	Passau	22	16
Freiberg	80	126	Potsdam	109	213
Freiburg	598	786	Regensburg	403	458
Gießen	284	357	Rostock	271	286
Göttingen	600	607	Saarbrücken	154	206
Greifswald	103	169	Siegen	109	133
Hagen	40	81	Stuttgart	433	566
Halle-Wittenberg	378	416	Trier	56	42
Hamburg	582	899	Tübingen	694	853
Hamburg Bundeswehr	24	12	Ulm	608	590
Hamburg Harburg	104	59	Weimar	17	3
Hannover	840	731	Wuppertal	95	189
Heidelberg	853	1115	Würzburg	657	806

Appendix 9: Overview of Publication Activity of all German Universities in absolute Numbers, 2009 (own illustration).

Overview of Publication Activity of all German Universities in absolute Numbers, 2009 (Differences in Size are not considered)					
University	Single-Authorship	Co-Authorship	University	Single-Authorship	Co-Authorship
Aachen RWTH	1201	1953	Hildesheim	21	22
Augsburg	137	289	Hohenheim	145	268
Bamberg	54	87	Ilmenau	132	287
Bayreuth	252	608	Jena	472	1236
Berlin FU	338	955	Kaiserslautern	212	447
Berlin Humboldt	301	1081	Kassel	143	279
Berlin TU	501	1396	Kiel	478	1260
Bielefeld	305	566	KIT	1006	2027
Bochum	710	1522	Koblenz-Landau	68	112
Bonn	782	2147	Köln	637	1707
Braunschweig	327	793	Konstanz	251	466
Bremen	489	1013	Leipzig	563	1463
Chemnitz	153	313	Lübeck	252	666
Clausthal	135	252	Lüneburg	24	46
Cottbus	41	107	Magdeburg	180	616
Darmstadt	536	1078	Mainz	432	1320
Dortmund	378	696	Mannheim	178	374
Dresden	779	1930	Marburg	310	846
Duisburg-Essen	641	1455	München Bundeswehr	48	93
Düsseldorf	339	907	München LMU	824	2651
Eichstädt-Ingolstadt	33	39	München TU	1155	3137
Erfurt	24	21	Münster	634	1541
Erlangen-Nürnberg	963	1992	Oldenburg	133	334
Flensburg	10	11	Osnabrück	118	323
Frankfurt	433	1336	Paderborn	213	345
Frankfurt Oder	17	20	Passau	39	63
Freiberg	102	198	Potsdam	268	610
Freiburg	757	1856	Regensburg	489	1106
Gießen	347	894	Rostock	466	844
Göttingen	597	1688	Saarbrücken	262	752
Greifswald	152	539	Siegen	127	287
Hagen	51	310	Stuttgart	517	1185
Halle-Wittenberg	346	784	Trier	66	179
Hamburg	660	1943	Tübingen	734	1798
Hamburg Bundeswehr	6	13	Ulm	513	1371
Hamburg Harburg	175	243	Weimar	50	54
Hannover	1050	1878	Wuppertal	130	441
Heidelberg	1072	3053	Würzburg	530	1408

Appendix 10: Table of Regression Results concerning scientific Publications.

Source	SS	df	MS
Model	97337.3889	8	12167.1736
Residual	42519.0551	295	144.13239
Total	139856.444	303	461.572423

Number of obs =	304
F(8, 295) =	84.42
Prob > F =	0.0000
R-squared =	0.6960
Adj R-squared =	0.6877
Root MSE =	12.006

pub	Coef.	Std. Err.	t	P>|t|	[95% Conf.	Interval]
Invest	1.67e-08	2.96e-08	0.56	0.574	-4.16e-08	7.49e-08
admIncome	2.32e-07	4.47e-08	5.20	0.000	1.44e-07	3.20e-07
thirdPF	2.22e-07	2.44e-08	9.09	0.000	1.74e-07	2.70e-07
Prof	-.0042077	.0052153	-0.81	0.420	-.0144716	.0060562
dummyelite	-.5111239	2.268074	-0.23	0.822	-4.97478	3.952532
dummytu	2.417128	2.169247	1.11	0.266	-1.852032	6.686287
dummymed	2.488651	1.751321	1.42	0.156	-.9580156	5.935318
dummysize	4.146088	2.383068	1.74	0.083	-.5438798	8.836057
_cons	-.3503321	1.684827	-0.21	0.835	-3.666135	2.965471

Appendix 11: Table of Regression Results concerning Patent Applications.

Source	SS	df	MS
Model	14894.04	8	1861.755
Residual	21320.0094	295	72.2712182
Total	36214.0493	303	119.518315

Number of obs =	304
F(8, 295) =	25.76
Prob > F =	0.0000
R-squared =	0.4113
Adj R-squared =	0.3953
Root MSE =	8.5012

pat	Coef.	Std. Err.	t	P>|t|	[95% Conf.	Interval]
Invest	1.78e-09	2.12e-08	0.08	0.933	-4.00e-08	4.36e-08
admIncome	2.61e-08	3.15e-08	0.83	0.407	-3.58e-08	8.81e-08
thirdPF	7.39e-08	1.84e-08	4.02	0.000	3.77e-08	1.10e-07
Profs	-.0017717	.0020612	-0.86	0.391	-.0058283	.0022849
dummyelite	7.592125	1.601903	4.74	0.000	4.439519	10.74473
dummytu	.7033047	1.5382	0.46	0.648	-2.323932	3.730542
dummymed	-1.353875	1.245715	-1.09	0.278	-3.805489	1.097739
dummysize	2.814059	1.637031	1.72	0.087	-.4076804	6.035798
_cons	.848239	1.098727	0.77	0.441	-1.314097	3.010575

Appendix 12: Overview of Fourfold Tables regarding the Collaboration Activity of the three Groups of German Universities, weighted Numbers, 2000 and 2009 (own illustration).

Overview of Fourfold-Tables regarding the Collaboration Activity of the three Groups of German Universities, 2000 and 2009 (weighted Numbers)

Fourfold Table regarding the Collaboration Activity, 2000, weighted Numbers (Elite vs. Non-Elite)				
		Single-Authorship	Co-Authorship	
		0	1	Total
Elite	0	8814	11126	19940
Non-Elite	1	14825	18127	32952
Total		23639	29253	52892
P-Value		*0,11475*		

Fourfold Table regarding the Collaboration Activity, 2009, weighted Numbers (Elite vs. Non-Elite)				
		Single-Authorship	Co-Authorship	
		0	1	Total
Elite	0	10141	25315	35456
Non-Elite	1	17918	43696	61614
Total		28059	69011	97070
P-Value		*0,112630003*		

Fourfold Table regarding the Collaboration Activity, 2000, weighted Numbers (TU vs. Non-TU)				
		Single-Authorship	Co-Authorship	
		0	1	Total
TU	0	6229	7153	13382
Non-TU	1	17410	22100	39510
Total		23639	29253	52892
P-Value		*5,94813E-07*		

Fourfold Table regarding the Collaboration Activity, 2009, weighted Numbers (TU vs. Non-TU)				
		Single-Authorship	Co-Authorship	
		0	1	Total
TU	0	8448	18013	26461
Non-TU	1	19611	50998	70609
Total		28059	69011	97070
P-Value		*5,38562E-37*		

Fourfold Table regarding the Collaboration Activity, 2000, weighted Numbers (Med vs. Non-Med)				
		Single-Authorship	Co-Authorship	
		0	1	Total
Med	0	18675	22743	41418
Non-Med	1	4964	6510	11474
Total		23639	29253	52892
P-Value		*0,000498668*		

Fourfold Table regarding the Collaboration Activity, 2009, weighted Numbers (Med vs. Non-Med)				
		Single-Authorship	Co-Authorship	
		0	1	Total
Med	0	21133	52807	73940
Non-Med	1	8000	16204	24204
Total		29133	69011	98144
P-Value		*7,15615E-40*		

Appendix 13: Overview of Fourfold Tables regarding the institutional Distribution of the Co-Authors of the three Groups of German Universities, weighted Numbers, 2000 and 2009 (own illustration).

Overview of Fourfold Tables regarding the institutional Distribution of Co-Authors of the three Groups of German Universities, 2000 and 2009 (weighted Numbers)

Fourfold Table regarding the institutional Distribution, 2000, weighted Numbers (Elite vs. Non-Elite)				
		Enterprises	Research Community	
		0	1	Total
Elite	0	316	4911	5227
Non-Elite	1	528	8231	8759
Total		844	13142	13986
P-Value		*0,966561851*		

Fourfold Table regarding the institutional Distribution, 2009, weighted Numbers (Elite vs. Non-Elite)				
		Enterprises	Research Community	
		0	1	Total
Elite	0	915	11147	12062
Non-Elite	1	1589	19193	20782
Total		2504	30340	32844
P-Value		*0,842821262*		

Fourfold Table regarding the institutional Distribution, 2000, weighted Numbers (TU vs. Non-TU)				
		Enterprises	Research Community	
		0	1	Total
TU	0	289,8233014	3239,233527	3529,057
Non-TU	1	556,3048824	9903,655387	10459,96
Total		846,1281838	13142,88891	13989,02
P-Value		*4,47815E-10*		

Fourfold Table regarding the institutional Distribution, 2009, weighted Numbers (TU vs. Non-TU)				
		Enterprises	Research Community	
		0	1	Total
TU	0	869	7909	8778
Non-TU	1	1634	22432	24066
Total		2503	30341	32844
P-Value		*5,4259E-21*		

Fourfold Table regarding the institutional Distribution, 2000, weighted Numbers (Med vs. Non-Med)				
		Enterprises	Research Community	
		0	1	Total
Med	0	613	10063	10676
Non-Med	1	232	3078	3310
Total		845	13141	13986
P-Value		*0,007507563*		

Fourfold Table regarding the institutional Distribution, 2009, weighted Numbers (Med vs. Non-Med)				
		Enterprises	Research Community	
		0	1	Total
Med	0	1817	23553	25370
Non-Med	1	687	6788	7475
Total		2504	30341	32845
P-Value		*6,29954E-09*		

Appendix 14: Overview of Fourfold Tables regarding the institutional Distribution of the Co-Applicants of the three Groups of German Universities, absolute Numbers, 1999/2000 and 2007/2008 (own illustration).

Overview of Fourfold Tables regarding the institutional Distribution of Co-Applicants of the three Groups of German Universities, 1999/2000 and 2007/2008 (absolute Numbers)

Fourfold Table regarding the institutional Distribution of the Co-Applicants, 1999/2000, absolute Numbers (Elite vs. Non-Elite)

		Enterprises	Research Community	
		0	1	Total
Elite	0	13	43	56
Non-Elite	1	15	124	139
Total		28	167	195
P-Value		0,02521		

Fourfold Table regarding the institutional Distribution of the Co-Applicants, 2007/2008, absolute Numbers (Elite vs. Non-Elite)

		Enterprises	Research Community	
		0	1	Total
Elite	0	65	98	163
Non-Elite	1	122	178	300
Total		187	276	463
P-Value		0,86869		

Fourfold Table regarding the institutional Distribution of the Co-Applicants, 1999/2000, absolute Numbers (TU vs. Non-TU)

		Enterprises	Research Community	
		0	1	Total
TU	0	17	41	58
Non-TU	1	14	137	151
Total		31	178	209
P-Value		0,00026		

Fourfold Table regarding the institutional Distribution of the Co-Applicants, 2007/2008, absolute Numbers (TU vs. Non-TU)

		Enterprises	Research Community	
		0	1	Total
TU	0	60	70	130
Non-TU	1	129	211	340
Total		189	281	470
P-Value		0,10432		

Fourfold Table regarding the institutional Distribution of the Co-Applicants, 1999/2000, absolute Numbers (Med vs. Non-Med)

		Enterprises	Research Community	
		0	1	Total
Med	0	13	146	159
Non-Med	1	18	32	50
Total		31	178	209
P-Value		1,378E-06		

Fourfold Table regarding the institutional Distribution of the Co-Applicants, 2007/2008, absolute Numbers (Med vs. Non-Med)

		Enterprises	Research Community	
		0	1	Total
Med	0	144	204	348
Non-Med	1	43	71	114
Total		187	275	462
P-Value		0,48959		

Appendix 15: Exemplary Illustration of all Network Interactions between the KIT and the German Universities that have been Subject of Study (in Terms of Publications, 2009).[79]

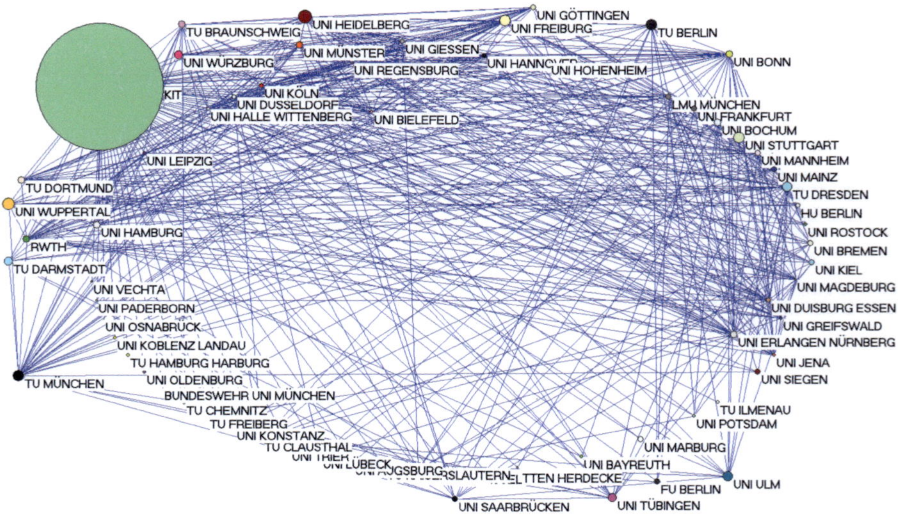

---

[79] It is not possible to properly visualize the whole network of the KIT as it is too large.

Appendix 16: Exemplary Illustration of all Network Interactions between the University of Heidelberg and the German Universities that have been Subject of Study (in Terms of Publications, 2009).[80]

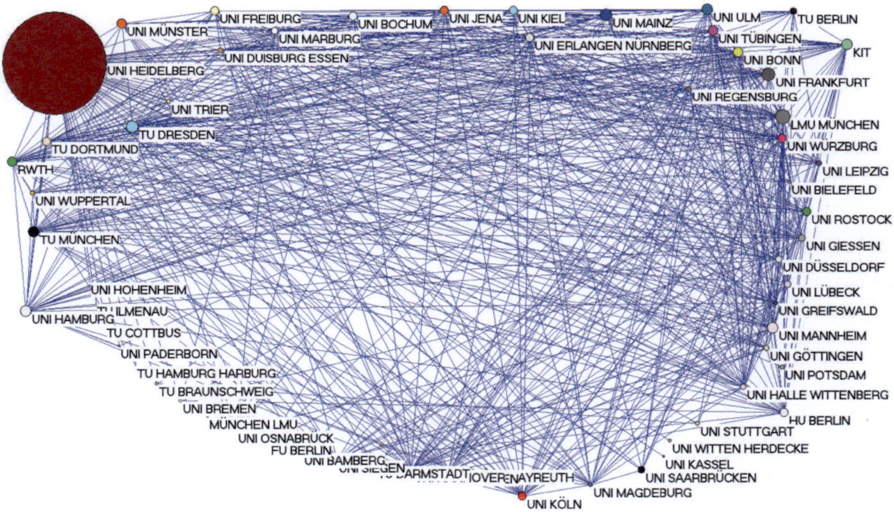

---

[80] It is not possible to properly visualize the whole network of the University of Heidelberg as it is too large.